NOTES

ON

THE ORGANISATION, METHODS, AND PROCESSES OF THE

PHOTO.-LITHO. OFFICE,

CALCUTTA

BY

MAJOR W. C. HEDLEY, R.E.

THIRD EDITION.

PUBLISHED UNDER THE DIRECTION OF THE SURVEYOR GENERAL OF INDIA.

CALCUTTA,
PRINTED BY THE PHOTO.-LITHO. OFFICE, SURVEY OF INDIA,
1924.

PREFACE TO FIRST EDITION.

These notes do not profess to give a complete account of the work in the Photo.-Litho. Office. They are intended primarily to assist an officer, who is new to the work, by explaining the organisation of the office, by drawing attention to those points which most tend to efficiency, and by laying down as far as possible the staff which is required and the rate of progress which should be attained.

They also form a record of the formulæ and processes in use in 1908. No formula or process can ever be looked upon as final: they are liable to constant change as improved methods are introduced; unless, however, accurate records are maintained of the methods in use in the office much valuable information will be lost and steady progress is impossible. For the formulæ here given I am primarily indebted to Mr. Vandyke and Mr. Taylor. The other instructions in this paper represent my own opinions, based on my experience at the Ordnance Survey Office, Southampton, and in the Photo.-Litho. Office.

CALCUTTA,   W. C. H.
August 5, 1908.

PREFACE TO SECOND EDITION.

The formulæ herein contained and the notes on the various processes are revised with additions and reprinted from the pamphlet entitled "Notes on the Organization, Methods and Processes of the Photo.-Litho. Office, Calcutta," by Major W. C. Hedley, R.E., first printed and published in 1908.

They are not intended in the nature of a report, but to constitute a record of the formulæ and processes in use in 1914 and to show such progress as has been made since the first edition was written.

Details have been so amplified as is hoped may render the work also of use to other reproducing offices.

My thanks are due to Mr. Taylor and Mr. Colquhoun for their valuable assistance.

CALCUTTA,   S. W. S. H.
October 1st 1924.

PREFACE TO THIRD EDITION.

These "Notes" are explanatory only; the work of the Photo.-Litho. Office is governed by Map Publication Orders and Photo.-Litho. Office Orders.

The present edition is rendered necessary by many minor changes in organisation and processes. Some details of procedure in the reproduction of Departmental maps have been omitted, as that subject is dealt with now by "Map Reproduction"—Chapter X of the Handbook of Topography. My thanks are due to Messrs. Colquhoun, Oddy, and Vandyke, and to the Head Clerk, Hari Prasad Sen, for their great help in the revision.

CALCUTTA,   F. J. M. K.

   1924.

CONTENTS.

ORGANISATION.

1. The Photo.-Litho. Office is under the Officer in charge and is divided into two Departments, Photographic and Lithographic, each of which has its own Manager and Assistant Manager.

These Departments are again divided into Sections each under its own Head Assistant; the various Sections are given below:—

Photographic Department.—

> Negative Section.
> Powder Section.
> Retouching (or Duffing) Section.
> Helio Section.
> Vandyke Section.
> Process-engraving Section.
> Negative Storing Section.

Lithographic Department.—

> Proving Section.
> Litho.-drawing Section.
> Machine Printing Section.
> Despatching Section.
> Graining Section.
> Type Printing Section.
> Plate and Stone Storing Section.

Each Manager has a small office consisting of one or more technical clerks for the purpose of registering all receipts and despatches in and from their respective Departments and the maintenance of the necessary card indexes for the efficient tracing of all work dealt with.

In addition to the above there is the main office (under the Head Clerk) and the Stores Section (under the Chief Store-keeper) both of which are directly responsible to the Officer in charge.

2. The technical establishment consists of *First Division* officers, mostly recruited by the Secretary of State, as being experts in their trades; *Second Division* officers, mainly selected men from the *Third Division*, which is recruited locally; and a large *Inferior Estabilshment*.

The First Division consists of the Managers' and Assistant Managers' posts; most of the Second Division officers are Head Assistants in charge of sections; the Third Division consists almost entirely of workers with their own hands, though there is no bar to a good Third Division man being in charge of a small section such as the Vandyke or Powder sections. The Inferior Establishment comprises such men as Machine feeders, Type inkmen, and labourers. For details of the 1908 Reorganisation, see Appendix VI.

Duties of the Officer in charge.

3. It must be the object of every officer administering the Photo.-Litho. Office, or indeed any other office, to know his men personally, to encourage the good and to keep back the bad ones. If he can do this, efficiency will result. He now has full powers to select and push on the best men, and to promote or keep back his whole staff according to their deserts. He must judge his men by the quality and quantity of the work which they turn out, and his own knowledge of all the various trades and processes should be sufficient to enable him to do this. It is not probable that his knowledge of each trade will be equal to that of the best men in those trades, nor is it necessary. It is however essential that he should know the results which can be obtained from each process, and the quantity and quality of the work which should be turned out by each man, and by each machine. He should in short be a good critic.

The Officer in charge should, subject to instructions received from the Director, Map Publication, decide on the method of reproduction of all maps; he should see and criticise all important proofs; he should see that work passes steadily through the office and that none is lost sight of; he should especially be careful that promises are not made which cannot be kept, and that when made they are kept; he should carefully supervise the annual indent for stores; he should watch the progress of each section, and see that none are blocked with work; he should carefully watch the outturn of the machines; he should enforce cleanliness and punctuality throughout the office.

One of the great difficulties in the Photo.-Litho. Office is to hold the proper balance between departmental and extra-departmental work. Extra-departmental work, if accepted, must be completed within a reasonable time. Departmental work must have the first place and only when that work is being turned out with sufficient speed should outside work be undertaken.

Every man who joins the department should be thoroughly taught his trade. Too much attention cannot be paid to this point. Apprentices should be given every chance; they should be taught, and not left to themselves. If they show no aptitude, the sooner they are discharged the better. It is fatal to the Department, and no kindness to the man himself, to retain him when he is unfitted for the work.

Duties of Managers and Assistant Managers.

4. The Managers and Assistant Managers, Photo. and Litho. should have a complete practical working knowledge of all the processes in use in their respective departments. They are not required as a rule to work with their own hands, but they should be able to do so, and they should be able personally to work each process better than any of their subordinates. The Manager, Photo., should be the best photographer; the Manager, Litho. should be the best printer. They are appointed to supply that expert knowledge which can only be acquired by years of practical work and experience, and are responsible to the Officer in charge for the efficiency of their departments. They should go round their departments regularly and personally know each man and his work. They should keep themselves up to date by study and be continually on the look out for any means of increasing the efficiency of their departments either by better processes or improved organisation.

Stock of plates and glasses will be taken twice yearly and checked with the books. The books will be put up for the signature of the Officer in charge on January 1st and July 1st.

5. Register Slips.—All orders for work are received from the Director, Map Publication (D. M. P.) on Register Slips and any further instructions are issued thereon by the Officer in charge Photo.-Litho. Office. **The instructions should be quite complete and should contain no reference to other papers. The importance of accurate, clear, and complete instructions cannot be over-estimated.**

The Register Slip number should appear as a press imprint on all departmental maps, and on all extra-departmental maps for which there is a possibility of a reprint being called. This press imprint of the Register Slip number will be shown in blue by No. 1. D. O. on all departmental maps and will be printed by the Photo.-Litho. Office in black; addition will be made for each reprint thus :—

Reg. No. 4751 D'12 (N.C. 2) 500—1,500 '17—1000'19.

Specimen copies of footnotes of departmental maps should be kept up to date by the Manager of the Photo. Branch, who is responsible for bringing to notice any irregularities or omissions in this respect in the orders on the Register Slip.

When a reprint of a departmental map is odered the Surveyor General's imprint and date will not be altered except in the case of a new edition, even though re-photography is necessary.

A reprint note will be added in the case of all reprints the wording for which note will be entered by the D. M. P. on the Register Slip.

The cost of work done by the Photo.-Litho. Office, which is to be billed for by the Map Record and Issue Office, should be clearly stated in the order or note on the Register Slip, written when the work is completed and sent to the Map Record and Issue Office for despatch.

Care should be taken that the total amount includes the cost of the various stages through which the job has passed, and does not include any sum which has already been billed for before.

It frequently happens that when a map, which has been previously published, is reprinted, the cost of the reprint is not clearly shown separately from that of the previous publication: it is essential that it should be separately shown so that no mistake may be made in the bill for the reprint.

PHOTOGRAPHIC DEPARTMENT.

6. The most important work of the office still remains the reproduction of the one-inch coloured map of India.

7. Negative Section.—The Negative Section does not take a photograph unless the dimensions to which the map is to be reproduced are given on the R.S.

Absolute accuracy in this respect is essential, and it is also essential that for maps for which two or more negatives are made, they should all be precisely the same size. Negatives are examined and, when passed, are initialled by the Manager or Assistant Manager, Photo. but the Head Assistant in charge of the Negative Section is responsible that the negatives are correct as to dimensions before the originals are taken down from the plan board.

When originals are in more than one piece great care is required to join them up accurately in their correct position. If the original is on one sheet of paper, all that is necessary is to see that headings and footnotes are complete and correct—for this and all else in the Negative Section the Head Assistant is responsible.

For our new style departmental maps in colours the Negative Section makes only one negative of the outline and one of the contours. These negatives are made "direct," i. e., without using a prism on the camera lens. Only moderate density is required; moreover, the intensification tends to obliterate the finer lines. With very slight intensification, and a final powdering with graphite when the negative is dry, it is possible to obtain a negative of sufficient density which still retains all the fine work.

The Cameras now in the Negative Section are as follows:—

No. 1 Camera.—Originally "Calcutta" pattern by Penrose & Co., but converted by M. I. O. to "Precision" type; takes a negative $46\frac{1}{2}'' \times 33''$.

> *Lenses.*—Zeiss apochromat "Planar" 1700 mm. (67″) focus, which would probably cover $50'' \times 40''$, if stopped down.
>
> Zeiss "Protar" 1310 mm. (52″) focus, which covers $42'' \times 28''$ when stopped down to F. 45.

No. 2 Camera.—Penrose "Precision" type, with half-tone screen gear; takes a negative $36'' \times 36''$.

Lens.—Cooke, 43″ focus.

No. 3 Camera.—Originally Penrose "Practical" type with half-tone screen gear but converted to "Precision" type by M. I. O.; takes a negative $30'' \times 24''$.

> *Lenses.*—Cooke, 42″ focus.
>
> Ross-Zeiss apochromatic "Tessar", 33″ focus.

No. 4 Camera.—Penrose "Precision" type with half-tone screen gear; takes a negative $30'' \times 24''$.

Lens.—Cooke 42″ focus.

No. 5 Camera.—Office-built $12'' \times 10''$, box camera.

Lens.—"Cooke," 18″ focus.

There is also a spare camera in store and for which there is no space in which to erect it. Its description is as follows.

Camera.—Penrose's Practical Camera without screen gear; takes a negative $30'' \times 24''$ extension 3 feet.

Lens.—Cooke 30″ focus.

One operator, *i.e.* a workman capable of doing all the operations involved in taking a negative from start to finish, is required for each camera, with two coolies. It is advantageous to have an apprentice at the large camera, as it is impossible for the operator to do the scaling single-handed.

In a 6-hour working day the number of negatives varies from 4 to 5 on No. 1 and No. 2 cameras, and from 3 to 4 the smaller cameras.

The following are the details of the half-tone screens in use in the Negative Section.—

$30'' \times 24''$ 133 lines to the inch (Max Levy.)
$22'' \times 20''$ 100   ,,   ,,   ,,
$24'' \times 19''$ "Metzgraph" Screen.

8. Powder Section.—Here contact prints are made from the camera negatives on to glass plates specially prepared, the result being any required number of reversed "powder" negatives. These prints are made by exposure to sunlight or electric arc lamps, the former being preferable.

The Section can turn out over 30 powder negatives in a six-hour day in good weather. It can more than keep pace with the cameras. The personnel consists of five operators and three coolies.

9. Retouching (or Duffing) Section.—The powder negatives are passed on to this section, where they are duffed for colours, &c.

The Section is responsible that the negatives are duffed in accurate accordance with the colour patterns, but it is not their duty to examine the correctness of the patterns by comparison with the originals, and the Photo.-Litho. Office has no responsibility for any errors arising from their incorrectness.

The Section consists of glass engravers, negative touchers and duffers. A glass engraver is a man who can draw and write on the negative. A negative toucher can strengthen and touch up weak parts of the negative and draw easy work. A duffer can merely paint out defects, or work which is not required, with his brush.

The duffing medium made up of Indian ink, ox-galls, carbolic acid, and distilled water may be replaced by Photo-pake, manufactured by the Vanguard Company. Care must be taken that Photopake is thoroughly stirred before use. One coat ensures absolute opacity and it can be washed off without injury to the negative. When first used it was found that it was attacked on the negative by insects, white ants, &c., and was also very sensitive to climatic changes and since 1912 it has therefore been mixed with glycerine and carbolic acid. So far as can at present be seen the negatives duffed with this medium will keep an indefinite period.

After the duffing and touching has been completed the negatives are examined before being sent for the preparation of the helio plates.

The completion of the colour negatives of an average one-inch sheet takes about fifteen working days; sheets on smaller scales and which are consequently, as rule, more complicated take proportionately longer.

10. Helio Section.—At first sight there does not appear to be much difficulty in making a helio but this is far from being the case. There is all the difference in the world between a good and a bad workman. Correct exposure is of course necessary but the skill seems to come in chiefly in the touch with which the ink is removed. With coloured maps, it is essential to get the lines and especially the names as clear and sharp as possible. The fine lines must not be lost and the thick lines must not be coarse. The attainment of this result requires much skill. The important plates are the black outline and the hills. With very close contours the fine ones must not be coarse; it is far better that some of them should be lost. A mass of coarse contours obscures all other detail.

Each helio printer should be capable of carrying out all the operations from the coating of the plate to the production of the finished article. Until a man can do this he is not classed as a trained helio. printer, though in actual practice it is found more advantageous to employ one man exclusively to carry out the work of each particular stage.

The present average rate of progress is 36 plates per six-hour day. Exposure to sunlight reflected from a mirror gives the best results, but arc lamps for printing have now been installed, and work can therefore be carried on in all weathers though the exposure takes somewhat longer when the arc lamps are used.

Freshly grained plates should be insisted on and any defects in the zinc or graining at once reported. No good work can be done with a badly grained plate.

11. Vandyke Section.—The supply of work for this section is intermittent. The men employed in the helio. section are also trained in the working of the Vandyke process so that they can be employed as required. The staff of the section is 2 operators and 3 coolies, and they can turn out 20 plates a day, given good light.

12. Process-engraving Section.—In years past much admirable work has been done by this Section, chiefly in the photogravure process. With the exception of the various weather charts in use throughout India which are now printed entirely from line blocks it has nothing whatever to do with the production of maps.

The photogravure work is being continued and the same high standard of quality maintained. Since the installation of a complete set of the machinery necessary for the rapid completion of half-tone and line blocks, the half-tone process has however gradually come more into use and this work now forms the chief work of the Section.

A good deal of bromide and a small amount of ferrotype (blue) printing is done.

Since the arrival of the Victoria platen machine and the Centurette machine, all the half-tone and line block printing is done in the Section.

The Section is capable of turning out on the average 4 deep etched and 30 fine etched half-tone and line blocks, 50 flat etched half-tone blocks and about 4 photogravure plates in a month.

The engraving of any lettering required on photogravure plates is carried out by the Engraving Office. Photogravure plates are proved in the Process-engraving Section but the plates are steel-faced and the copies printed off in the Engraving Office.

This Section has it's own studio which contains the following cameras:—

1 "Precision" process camera, 15″ × 15″, by Messrs. A. W. Penrose.

Lens :—18″ focus Process lens by Cooke.

1 "Precision" process camera, 15″ × 12″, by Messrs. A. W. Penrose.

Lens:—18″ focus Process lens by Cooke.

1 camera, 15″ × 12″ by G. Hare.
1 camera, 10″ × 18″ by G. Hare.
1 camera, 5″ × 4″ by Stanley.
7 other lenses of sorts.

The following half-tone screens are in use:—

2 150-line screens, 15″ × 12″, by Max Levy.
1 175-line screen, 12″ × 10″, by Max Levy.
1 120-line screen, 12″ × 10″, by Max Levy.
1 Metzograph screen, 15″ × 12″.

The following machines are used for printing half-tone and line blocks:—

1 "Centurette" double crown size, by the Linotype and Machinery Company.
1 "Victoria" Platen, foolscap size by Rockstroh & Schneider Nachf, Dresden.
1 "Laureate" Platen, foolscap size by Walker Bros., London.

There is one copper plate press by Benjamin Winstone, which is used for proving photogravure plates, and one small hand press by R. Hoe & Co., for proving half-tone and line blocks.

The following miscellaneous machines are also in use :—

1 Routing machine by Messrs. Royle, London.
1 Bevelling machine by Messrs. Royle, London.
1 power-driven circular saw by Messrs. A. W. Penrose.
1 "Acid-blast" etching machine by Max Levy.

LITHOGRAPHIC DEPARTMENT.

13. We now leave the Photo. Department and pass on to the Litho. Register Slips (R. S.) with originals and colour patterns are sent to the Manager, Litho. and the helio plates are sent direct to the Proving Section.

The originals and colour patterns are sent on to the Drawing Section, where they remain till the work is completed, but are always available for reference by other sections.

14. Proving Section.—The number of hand presses in use for proving is 16 :—4 Double Imperial, 8 Double Elephant, and 4 Imperial size. Twelve presses are continually in use, while the remaining four are used for stone work or when any of the others break down.

One printer, one spongeman and two pressmen are employed on each of the twelve larger presses, while the Imperial size presses are worked with one printer and two pressmen.

The first duty of the Proving Section is to supply black proofs of every plate it receives to the Litho.-drawing Section for examination.

The plates should be proved as soon as possible after their receipt from the Photo. Department, for they are not gummed up either in the Helio or Vandyke Sections and will therefore deteriorate if not quickly proved. Once black proofs for examination have been supplied, all future work depends on the instructions received from the head of the Drawing Section.

In addition to the preliminary proofs called for on the Register Slip, 3 black prints on art paper of the complete outline and contour plates of all $1''$, $\frac{1}{2}''$, $\frac{1}{4}''$ and $\frac{1}{M}$ sheets will be prepared in the Photo.-Litho. Office and stored with the originals of the sheets in the Map Record and Issue Office. In the case of $1''$ and $\frac{1}{2}''$ maps four reductions of the complete outline and contours in black on bankpost paper are also sent with the preliminary proofs for use in the Office Copy Section of the Drawing Office.

The charge for transfers of Departmental maps supplied to private firms will be Rs. 32 for a single transfer. If the map is on more than one stone or plate the charge for each transfer after the first will be at the Office rate for proving.

Absolute cleanliness should be observed in proving. Dirty sponges, rollers, etches, &c., are fatal to good work. Care should be taken that a plate is properly prepared before transferring, and proofs of colour maps should be easily intelligible patterns for examination and for the machine printer.

Too much proving should be avoided, as it tends to spoil the plates; a natural result of having to dry the plates for each proof; therefore as few proofs as possible should be pulled for examination. It is better to send a proof for examination a little out of register than to re-prove.

A weak plate can be strengthened by washing out with bitumen mixture and leaving it for 24 hours. Coarse work can often be much improved by etching.

It is of the utmost importance that plates should be properly prepared when being put away. When temporarily laid aside it is sufficient to ink them up and gum them, but when finally stored they should be put away in bitumen.

15. Litho.-drawing Section.—This section includes litho. draftsmen, zinc correctors and proof examiners.

A litho. draftsman is a man who can draw or write reversed on stone. If he can only touch up he should be called a corrector, not a draftsman.

Very little original work is now done on stone, but a small staff of first class litho. draftsmen is maintained. Draftsmen should take every precaution against spoiling a stone. It is an easy thing to do, especially when the ink on the stone is not copper-plate ink, which is a good acid resist. The acid used for the preparation of a stone for new work must not be stronger than one in fifty. It should cause very little, if any, effervescence on the stone. Two treatments with a weak acid are better than one with a strong. Acid must not be left on a stone too long and when removed it must be thoroughly washed off. All these points are well known but are sometimes neglected. To neglect them is probably to spoil the work.

Care should be taken that there should always be at least one draftsman capable of using the air brush.

Perfect cleanliness of all materials is essential to good work on stone.

A zinc corrector is a man who alters or corrects a zinc plate. The less a zinc plate is altered or corrected the better. Owing to the careful examination of the negatives and the power of correcting the negative and getting a new helio. at any time, the corrections on the zinc plates ought to be very few. There is however usually something to be done, and it is of the utmost importance that the plate should not be spoiled in the process.

Whenever a zinc plate is prepared with acid for alteration or the reception of new work there is a slight tendency for the lines to thicken. The important points to be attended to are—

(a) The acid should not be too strong.

(b) The acid must be thoroughly washed off and the plate blotted with clean blotting paper and fanned dry as quickly as possible.

(c) The less a plate is exposed in an ungummed state the better.

Gumming out a plate for the transfer of tints, &c., requires care, but it is very simple work and is usually done by the junior men and by apprentices; this work has been largely diminished by the introduction of methods by means of which tints are produced on plates photographically.

No hand-work whatever has to be done now on yellow plates for cultivation areas, while on green plates for forest areas the only hand-work is the drawing of the solid riband along the external boundaries of reserved forest areas.

The introduction of layered maps necessitated a great deal of gumming out for the transfer of tints until a photographic method of producing these tints was devised. By this method two out of the three tints, which each ordinary layer plate is required to print, are produced photographically on the plate so that the only work which remains to be done by hand is the painting in on the plate of the third—or solid—tint.

The Head Assistant in charge of the Litho.-drawing Section has one of the most important posts in the office, and he is responsible for the work of each of the three sub-sections. He receives proofs in black of all maps and plates, has them examined, and issues instructions to the Proving Section accordingly. He also receives coloured proofs of all maps in colour and is responsible for passing the proofs before the map is printed; it is for him to decide whether further proofs are necessary or not. He receives proofs in black of each plate of a coloured map and thenceforth controls the preparation of that map, until he passes the final proof.

As regards coloured one-inch maps, the Head Assistant of the Litho.-drawing Section receives a black proof of each plate, and it is his duty to decide, in consultation if necessary with the head of the Printing Section, whether the proofs are good enough.

If so, he calls for the necessary sets-off, and proceeds with the gumming out, after which the plates are sent to the Proving Section for transferring, and at the same time colour proofs of the map are asked for. The head of the Litho.-drawing Section should carefully preserve a black proof of each plate shewing all the corrections resulting from an examination of the colour proofs. If the corrections are heavy on any particular plate, the corrected proof should be sent to the Manager, Photo. to have the negative corrected and for the supply of a fresh helio.; minor corrections are carried out on the plate.

Formerly coloured proofs were not called for until the black proofs were examined and corrected. Coloured proofs only are now examined, thus avoiding double examination, and much saving of time and labour is gained. These proofs are finally passed by the O.C., P. L. O.

After the map is printed, *all* proofs of the negatives which have to be kept are sent to the Manager, Photo. who has the necessary corrections made on the negatives.

Too much importance cannot be attached to having all corrections plainly shewn on the proofs.

Proof examiners are not responsible for the correctness of originals or of colour patterns. They will point out errors if they detect them but should not spend their time looking for them. Their duty is to see that the reproduction corresponds with the originals and colour patterns and that the quality of the reproduction is good.

When several plates have been prepared by duffing negatives of the same original, a very careful examination of the colour proofs is necessary. This examination should be made from the colour pattern and not from the original, though the latter should be referred to in case any error is suspected. The negatives of these plates have already been examined, and if this work was properly done the corrections should be very small.

In all cases any errors found should be *very plainly* marked on the colour proofs for the information of the zinc correctors; when the negatives have to be kept these errors are also *very plainly* marked on the black proof for the subsequent correction of the negative.

The chief points to be attended to are as follows:—

    (1) The quality of the reproduction.

    (2) Registration.

    (3) See that no object is shown in two colours.

    (4) See that all footnotes, headings, &c., are complete.

    (5) See that the colours are the proper tint.

    (6) See that contour values are not super-imposed on detail of another colour.

The words "Uncorrected Proof" will be so stamped within the border of proof maps as to interfere as little as possible with the details in the body of the map.

16. Machine Printing Section.

The machines in use in order of size are given below:—

    No. 4 (Furnival & Co., 1904), Quad Demy; size of bed, Double Imperial.

    No. 1 (Furnival & Co., 1889), Quad Crown; size of bed, Double Imperial.

    No. 8 (Mann & Co., 1915), Quad Crown; size of bed, Double Imperial.

    No. 9 (Mann & Co., 1916), Quad Crown; size of bed, Double Imperial.

    No. 10 (Ratcliffe & Co., 1919), Double Demy; size of bed, 36″ × 24″.

    No. 7 (Mann & Co., 1914), Double Demy; size of bed, Imperial.

No. 2 (Furnival & Co., 1898), Double Demy; size of bed, Imperial.

No. 5 (Furnival & Co., 1907), Double Demy; size of bed, Imperial.

No. 6 (Mann & Co., 1912), Double Demy; size of bed, Imperial.

No. 3 (R. Hoe & Co., 1913), size of bed, Double Foolscap.

One printer, one layer-on (or an assistant under training as a printer), and 1 to 2 coolies are required for each machine.

The proper organisation of work in the machine room is essential to efficiency.

All plates should be washed out and inked up in a hand press before being put into the machine. A machine should be printing good impressions of a black map within a quarter of an hour of taking up the plate to put it in the machine.

All paper for colour work must be hung up in the machine room for at least 12 hours before printing. It must also be put through the machine before printing, for paper always stretches slightly the first time it goes through. For maps which have more than one printing it is desirable that the work on each plate should be as nearly as possible in the same position on the plate. This saves time in getting the correct lay, and is arranged for by the Helio. Section.

With paper which has been hung up and calendered there should not be much trouble with the registration of coloured maps. If necessary, however, recourse must be had to the dying box in the machine room. It is desirable that each machine printer should have a thorough knowledge of his machine and of the proper treatment of a stone or plate.

Each machine printer must keep a diary showing paper drawn and the maps printed.

Printers draw their own paper from the expense paper store. The percentage of wastage varies according to the number of colours and the length of the run. The rate of progress depends chiefly on the length of the run but is also affected by the size of the map—the smallar machines giving a quicker rate than the larger.

For a long run of a simple job in one colour on the smaller machines the outturn varies from 2,000 to 2,500 pulls in a Photo.-Litho. Office day, while on the larger machines the outturn is not usually more than 1,500 to 2,000; a good man will do two runs of 1,000 pulls each in a day on a small machine. The usual edition of the one-inch map in colours is 250, and one machine can print one colour of four different sheets in a day. Layered plates at present take about one-third as long again to print as ordinary plates.

The changing of colours on machines should be avoided as much as possible.

Each machine printer prepares his own plates for putting away after the completion of the printing and hands them over to the Plate-storing Section at the end of the day's work.

17. There are three minor duties in the Litho. Department which deserve a reference—

(*a*) Making transfer paper.

(*b*) Covering rollers.

(*c*) Making up etches, acids, &c.

Transfer paper may be made or bought ready made. It is usually made in the Photo.-Litho. Office from the formulæ laid down, but French transfer paper, which is transparent, is obtained from home and is useful. The formulæ are given in Appendix II. The point to emphasize is the necessity for absolute cleanliness. All jars when empty should be thoroughly washed inside and out, and the benches, &c., should be kept perfectly clean.

18. Type Printing Section.—This Section deals with the composition and printing of all handbooks, pamphlets and orders issued, and forms in use in the Survey of India, averaging some 250,000 impressions a month.

Its equipment consists of 6 machines, and 3 hand presses for proving, &c., and all necessary type and compositors' apparatus. One printer and one inkman are employed on each machine.

The methods are those in use in any ordinary type printing establishment and call for no special remark.

19. Despatching Section.—The examination here is of an entirely different kind to that expected from a proof examiner. It is of the most cursory kind and is merely directed to the following points :—

(a) That the number is correct.

(b) That the impressions are clean, without stains, untorn, and generally fit for issue.

(c) That the colours used are correct.

(d) That registration is approximately correct.

(e) The imprints for which the Photo.-Litho. Office are responsible should be examined on one impression.

The section is capable of keeping pace with the outturn of the office ; it keeps books showing—

(a) The impressions passed.

(b) Do. do. condemned.

These books are a most useful check on the printers.

The passed impressions are sent to the despatchers and the condemned ones destroyed after being seen by the Manager, Litho. All paper cutting and the trimming of impressions is also done in the Despatching Section which is provided with a cutting machine for the purpose.

One copy of each map or job completed will be submitted weekly to the Director, Map Publication, through the O.C., P. L. O. These copies will be returned by the Director, Map Publication with his remarks, if any and be filed in the Despatching Section.

When an extra-departmental map or plan of a town or portion of a town is printed, one copy will be sent by the Officer in Charge, Photo.-Litho. Office, to the Officer in charge, Map Record and Issue Office, to be filed in that office for reference only and not for issue.

20. Expense Paper Store.—Sufficient paper should be kept in the expense paper store to meet the current needs of the printers. About a fortnight's supply should be sufficient. Paper should be taken out of its wrapping and stored on a curved board such as those now in the store.

The store is kept by one man under the head of the Despatching Section.

21. Disposal of Documents.—On the completion of a map the documents are disposed of as follows :—

For Departmental maps—

(a) Originals with colour patterns and press order proof to M. R. I. O., in one envelope.

(b) Printed copies to M. R. I. O.

(c) One copy to D. M. P. through M. R. I. O. with the R. S.

(d) All other spare proofs and spoiled impressions are destroyed.

For Extra-departmental maps—

(a) Originals are disposed of as ordered on the R. S. or the file.

(b) In exceptional cases. the printed maps are despatched to their destination by the Photo.-Litho. Office, but they are generally sent to the M. R. I. O.

(c) One copy is filed with R. S., and one with the correspondence file. One copy of every extra-departmental map containing a town, or part of a town, is sent to the M. R. I. O. where it is filed for reference.

(d) All spare proofs or spoiled impressions are destroyed.

(e) The press order proof is returned to D. M. P. and filed by him.

The black proofs, showing the corrections which have been made to the negatives and plates, may be destroyed, as soon as the corrections have been carried out. (See 5th sub-para. on page 13).

22. Disposal of Negatives and Plates.—As soon as a map is printed, a decision is necessary as to whether negatives and plates are to be kept or cleaned off. The rules are as follows and are taken from D. M. P's. Order No. 88, of 23rd June 1919.

The following negatives and plates will be kept in the Photo.-Litho. Office and not cleaned off until superseded :—

I. *Negatives*—All negatives of secret maps and any Departmental or Extra-Departmental negatives which the Officer in charge, Photo.-Litho. Office, specially orders to be kept.

II. *Plates*— Combined-outline and hill plates of modern $1''$ and $\frac{1}{2}''$ sheets.

All plates of $1''$ and $\frac{1}{2}''$ sheets specially ordered by Officer in charge, Photo.-Litho. Office.

All plates of Mobilization "A" sheets.

All plates of *(a)* Secret maps.

„ *(b)* $\left\{ \begin{array}{l} \text{Degree sheets.} \\ \frac{1}{M} \text{ sheets.} \\ \frac{1}{2M} \text{ and smaller scale sheets.} \end{array} \right.$

„ *(c)* Manœuvre Areas.

„ *(d)* R. A. P. C. and R. A. F. Maps.

„ *(e)* Special maps of Cantonments and large towns.

„ *(f)* Town Guide Maps.

„ *(g)* E. D. Maps as specially ordered.

Secret and F. O. U. O. negatives and plates will be kept under lock and key.

All negatives and plates must be corrected before they are stored.

Otherwise all negatives and plates will be cleaned off after publication. For blue prints for survey or mapping the negatives will be cleaned off after supply of prints, and the plates on receipt of fair originals. These instructions are supplemented by P. L. O. Orders (Professional), which go into details.

The plates of all extra-departmental maps, plans, diagrams, &c., are dealt with at the discretion of the Officer in charge, Photo.-Litho. Office. When the nature of the work and the probable saving of time and labour in the future are such as to justify the keeping of the plates standing for a certain period, the Officer in charge, Photo.-Litho. Office, should decide what the duration of this period shall be.

In future, no undertaking will be made to keep the plates of any extra-departmental job standing in the Photo.-Litho. Office. Plates for the retention of which payment has been received, are cleaned off when they have been kept for five years.

The negatives and plates are kept in temporary racks until the final orders for their disposal are passed. On receipt of these orders the plates are transferred to the permanent racks and entered in the catalogue of plates. The same procedure holds good for the negatives, but a certificate, signed by the Manager, Photo., is added that the negatives have been corrected.

23. Plate Storing Section.—The work of this section is most important and if properly carried out saves endless time and trouble throughout the Litho. Branch.

Its Head is responsible that all plates are correctly numbered, entered up in the books, and stored on completion of work, and that all plates before being stored are properly put away in bitumen.

He is likewise responsible for the issue of all plates required for reprints, re-proving, &c.

He should maintain his books with such accuracy that he can at all times lay his hands on any plate immediately he is called upon to do so.

24. Graining Section.—It is the duty of the
Assistant in charge of the graining shed to see that all plates
are of a size to fit the beds of the machines.

These sizes are—

Double Imperial, $45'' \times 34''$.

Double Elephant, $42'' \times 31\frac{1}{2}''$.

Imperial, $32'' \times 24''$.

Double Foolscap, $26\frac{1}{2}'' \times 24''$.

Foolscap, $20'' \times 16''$.

These are the 5 sizes of plates in use and every plate
issued must be exactly one of these sizes.

All graining is done by machinery, electrically operated;
excellent results can be obtained by hand, but the results
by machinery are more uniform and the saving in labour
and time is very great. There are at present 4 machines
in use, all of which were obtained from England.

The graining is done with fine river sand, capable
of passing through a 120 mesh sieve, and water; the
graining action being done with either zinc balls or glass
marbles of about $\frac{3}{4}$ to 1 inch in diameter, made to move
in circles over the plate by the circular motion of the
machine. When the graining is complete the plate should
appear perfectly smooth, with an even matt surface. The
plate is then thoroughly well washed, back and front, the
surplus water squeegeed off, and the plate quickly dried
by heat. Rapid drying is essential and very important,
and a hot plate is provided for the purpose; otherwise the
surface becomes oxidised and will give trouble in the after
processes. An electric fan is also used to assist the drying when the humidity is very great.

No pains should be spared to get perfectly grained
plates, as the success of the work depends on it.

Old plates with work on them are first cleaned by washing off the ink with turpentine and then smearing over with
a strong solution of crude caustic potash (1 lb. caustic, 3
oz. water); this is followed by a solution of sulphuric acid
(1 to 5); the plate is then well washed and grained.

Plates must be freshly grained when used. All plates therefore which are sent to the Helio. or Vandyke Sections for use on a certain day, should be grained, or finally grained, the day before they are required. To ensure this being done, a sufficient stock of plates, whose graining is nearly complete, should always be kept; these can be finished off at short notice and issued as required.

The Assistant of the graining shed should always ascertain from the Manager, Photo., what plates he requires for the succeeding day, and these plates, freshly grained, should be sent to the Helio. or Vandyke Sections early on the morning of the day they are required; or if more convenient they may be sent the previous evening.

The Assistant of the graining shed keeps a book giving the following information:—

(1)   The number and sizes of new plates drawn from store.

(2)   The number and sizes of plates condemned and returned to store.

(3)   The number and sizes of grained plates issued daily.

The following staff is required:—

One Assistant in charge	
Each two machines, one coolie	... 2
Drying plates, one coolie ...	... 1
General assistant, one coolie ...	... 1
Cleaning off old work, two coolies	... 2
Polishing plates, two coolies ...	... 2
Total, one Assistant and 8 coolies.	

STORES SECTION.

25. The duties of the Chief Store-keeper (C. S. K.) are very important and are as follows:—

(a)   He is responsible for the safe custody of all unissued stores and for all furniture and fittings. He will take proper precautions for the safe keeping of all the keys.

(*b*) He maintains ledgers showing the receipt and issue of all stores. Stores are divided into alphabetical sections, for each of which a separate alphabetical ledger is kept; stock can thus be taken section by section without closing the whole of the stocks. Separate ledgers are kept for paper and type.

(*c*) All stores of every kind which come into the office are received by the Chief Store-keeper and entered in the ledgers. All stores are issued by him and receipt vouchers obtained. Without a voucher nothing is issued.

(*d*) Requisitions for stores are made out at regular periods, with occasional exceptions, by the heads of Sections and are checked before issue by the Managers, who sign for all stores and stock in their charge and are responsible for them. The Chief Store-keeper has no responsibility for any article for which he holds a receipt from a Manager.

(*e*) All stores, when no longer serviceable, are returned to the Chief Store-keeper and disposed of by him under the orders of the Officer in charge.

(*f*) It is the duty of the Chief Store-keeper to make himself thoroughly acquainted with the qualities of the stores which pass through his hands. He should keep records of those which have proved good or the reverse, and note the names of firms from whom satisfactory articles have been obtained. He should ascertain the wants of the working departments and see that his stores will be sufficient to meet them; he should know the best places to buy stores which have to be obtained locally, and should buy such stores in sufficient quantities to obtain a reduction in price; he should call for tenders from several firms and submit them to the Officer in charge before making a considerable purchase. A most important duty is the preparation of the annual indent for stores from home. He should be most careful to specify exactly what is required, and should always state in the margin what firm or firms have previously proved satisfactory or the reverse. Stores should be examined when received and a report sent to the India Office as soon as possible on any article which has been found defective. Every effort is made by the Director of Stores at the India Office to comply with our demands, but it is essential that those demands be clearly stated, and that any defects or deficiencies be promptly reported.

(g) The following are the books kept by the Chief Store-keeper.

(1) Store ledgers.

(2) Requisition book on M. I. O.

(3) Requisition book for repairs to be carried out by M. I. O.

(4) Bazar indent book.

(h) The Chief Store-keeper will also prepare the following periodical statements and submit them in time to reach the Director, Map Publication by the dates on which they are due.

(1) Annual indent on the Stationery Office, due on January 1st.

(2) Abstract estimate of value of stores required from England, for annual forecast. Due on August 1st.

(3) Annual indent for stores required from England. Due on August 15th.

(i) He will keep office copies of the above statements in separate files. All letters, Government of India Orders, Departmental Orders or Circulars, &c., relating to stores, are also to be filed separately and kept in his charge.

(*j*) All stores and other articles, should, immediately on receipt and entry in the store books, be marked with office stamp or labelled as Government property. The year of receipt should also be prominently marked on all stores.

(*k*) All almirahs and store rooms should be periodically cleaned out thoroughly and their contents overhauled to see that they are in good condition. Useless and worn-out stores should be kept apart and periodically disposed of under the orders of the Officer in charge, Photo.-Litho. Office

(*l*) The Chief Store-keeper is responsible for checking the stock in hand of all stores once a year, the stock-taking to be completed before the 31st of March. He is also responsible for bringing to the notice of the Officer in charge, Photo.-Litho. Office any discrepancies which may be noticed between the stock in hand and the ledger balances, and he is liable to make good any deficiencies. The Chief Store-keeper should sign and date opposite the balance of each item in the ledgers as a certificate as to its correctness. If the Chief Store-keeper deputes his assistant to check the balance in hand of any item, his assistant must initial and date the balance, and the Chief Store-keeper must sign as to its correctness.

(*m*) All stores such as paper, &c., which are liable to damage by damp or white ants must be so stored as to be kept off the floor.

(*n*) Old stock should be used up before new stock is issued; and stores which have gone out of use must be disposed of, under the orders of the Officer in charge, Photo.-Litho. Office.

(*o*) The stock of valuable stores such as silver
nitrate and iodine should be checked by the
Chief Store-keeper on the 1st of each month
and a certificate sent to the Officer in
charge, Photo.-Litho. Office that this has
been done.

(*p*) The Officer in charge, Photo.-Litho. Office will,
at irregular intervals, check a percentage of
the stock in the store godowns against the
ledgers, initialling and dating those items
which he has checked.

Appendix I.

FORMULÆ AND METHODS IN PHOTOGRAPHIC DEPARTMENT.

Glass Cleaning.

1. The negative glass is English polished patent plate $\frac{1}{4}''$ thick. It should be coated with grease, when sent out, to prevent oxidation.

2. New glass is cleaned with—

Caustic Potash	...	... 7 Kilos
Water ...	...	... 5 Litres

old negatives have the films removed with a solution of nitric acid.

Nitric acid	...	... 1,000 c. c.
Water ...	...	... 250 c. c.

If a little of the above solution is smeared over the surface of each negative and allowed to stand overnight, the films are removed quite easily the next morning with a piece of zinc.

Both sides and all edges of the glass should be well scrubbed to avoid any possibility of the presence of dirt contaminating the bath.

One coolie is sufficient for rough cleaning.

The glasses are polished with—

Tripoli powder	...	... 20 gms.
Spirits of wine	...	... 20 c. c.
Water ...	...	.. 500 c. c.

The polished side is then coated with a solution of—

Fluid egg albumen ...	...	... 60 c. c.
Water ...	...	... 500 c. c.
Liq. Ammonia 880°	...	... 10 c. c.
Alcohol	...	... 20 c. c.

If the solution appears cloudy a few drops of liq. ammonia are added. Dry albumen gives satisfactory results and is more convenient than fresh egg albumen. The solution should be well filtered, and the glasses flowed over twice and then placed on a rack to dry. If placed on the floor, dust runs up the glass and causes a scum. Two coolies can do all the glass cleaning.

Coating glass. Collodion.

The glasses are coated with collodion prepared according to the following formulæ.

Necoloidine collodion— For screen-making and stripping :—

Necoloidine	...	...	4 oz.
Ether ...	...	...	2½ litres.
Alcohol ...	...	...	2½ litres.

Cotton collodion—

Pyroxylin	...	...	4 oz.
(Hopkins & Williams)			
Ether ...	...	...	4,000 c. c.
Alcohol ...	...	...	2,000 c. c.

Collodion for use in the Indian climate must have superior characteristics :—

1. It must flow easily, to enable large plates to be evenly coated.

2. It must "set" *slowly* to give the operator time to coat the plate carefully.

3. It must have sufficient "body" and porosity to carry the largest amount of bath solution possible, so as to avoid drying in the camera during exposure.

Cotton or Pyroxylin collodion—

The pyroxylin is received from England in sealed jars, the jars being kept filled with water to minimise risk of fire or explosion. As received it is too acid for use, so the acidity is removed by washing. When it shows no trace of acidity it is dried and teased out, all lumps being carefully separated. The washed and teased cotton is then placed on a stretcher covered with muslin, and placed in the sun to dry. This drying is a most important point, as the slightest trace of moisture reduces the solubility of the pyroxylin and gives an opalescent instead of a clear collodion. For this reason it is always desirable to make collodion in dry sunny weather. The pyroxylin is then soaked in the required amount of alcohol until it is well swelled, the ether is then added and the pyroxylin dissolves forming a clear liquid.

Iodizer.

In the foregoing note on the manufacture of collodion the special qualities required are described, and how they are obtained explained. It must however be borne in mind that these qualities may be upset by the use of an unsuitable iodizer. The salts of cadmium have the property of thickening collodion, while those of ammonium thin it; thus the proportions of the two salts should be so balanced as to maintain the collodion at the same consistency as it is before iodizing. This is apart altogether from the photographic qualities of the salts mentioned, which require very careful adjustment. The iodides alone give good density and clearness, but require great cleanliness and care in use. The addition of bromide lengthens the range of gradation and renders the collodion more immune to impurities in the silver bath.

The proportion of ammonium to cadmium salt also determines the time in which the collodion will ripen. A collodion which ripens too quickly goes bad in a proportionate time. The iodizer below gives a collodion which ripens in about three days and will keep in good order for weeks.

Iodizer—

Alcohol ...	...	... 5,000 c. c.
Ammonium iodide	...	... 100 gms.
Cadmium iodide	...	... 60 ,,
,, bromide	...	... 40 ,,

The pyroxylin collodion and the iodizer are mixed as follows:—

For use in the hot weather—

Pyroxylin collodion ...	...	5,000 c. c.
Iodizer ...	...	... 750 c. c.

In the cold weather the proportion of iodizer is raised to 1,000 c. c. The collodion should not be used too fresh, but should be allowed to stand for at least three days after iodizing. A few drops of iodine solution are added at the time of iodizing. This is to prevent fog, which sometimes occurs through the want of sufficient free iodine in the collodion.

Half an ounce added to six litres of collodion is found to work well.

Iodine solution—

Iodine ...	...	... 5 gms.
Iodizer ...	...	... 500 c. c.

The collodion should be filtered. The coating bottle should not be quite full, and the excess from the glass should always be poured into a second bottle which should afterwards be carefully filtered back into the first bottle. The main points requiring attention in coating are to pour sufficient collodion on the glass at first in a circular pool, to tilt the glass gently from corner to corner, to rock well when pouring off, and to avoid hurry without unnecessary delay. If this operation is carefully and properly performed, there should be an even film of collodion free from all waviness.

Silver baths.

The excellence of a negative depends very largely on the condition of the sensitising bath.

This much maligned part of the wet collodion photographer's equipment requires a certain amount of care and intelligence in use. Given that, there is very little difficulty in successfully managing a silver bath. Cleanliness is of course a necessity, and every care should be taken that no impurities find their way into the bath. Glasses should be carefully cleaned, especially the edges, and dishes, funnels and bottles used for the silver bath should be strictly reserved for that purpose only.

The strengths of the baths used are in the hot weather 20 to 25 and in the cold weather 25 to 30 grains per ounce, acidified with chemically pure nitric acid as necessary.

To make up a new bath weigh out the required amount of silver nitrate, dissolve it in the smallest possible quantity of water, and add a few grains of potasium iodide; then add sufficient water to bring the bath to the required strength. The reason for adding the iodide is that nitrate of silver is a solvent of silver iodide, and if this is not added, the first few negatives will be lacking in density. The same result can be obtained by coating a plate with iodised collodion and leaving it in the bath for an hour.

A bath after being in use for some time becomes saturated with alcohol and ether; to get rid of this the bath may be put in an open glass or earthenware dish and evaporated till it crystallises, and then re-dissolved in distilled water, or it may be put in an evaporating basin and boiled; the latter is the quickest but not the best method. It should be borne in mind that before boiling down a strongly alcoholic bath it must be made *slightly* alkaline, otherwise there is a risk of the formation of fulminate of silver, a highly powerful explosive. The amount produced may be small but it is sufficient to break the evaporating basin and scatter boiling nitrate of silver over a radius of at least ten yards.

To treat a bath which does not require boiling down but is giving bad results, add pure ammonia *gradually* until it is just alkaline and *no more*, and place it in bright sunlight for a day or two; the silver then combines with any organic impurities in the bath and precipitates them as a black powder, which settles to the bottom of the bottle and can be filtered out. The bath is then re-acidified and is ready for use.

Each camera is supplied with three baths, one in use and two being "sunned;" by this means an operator has no occasion to lose time by his bath going wrong.

A bath in the hands of a careful operator will usually remain in good working order till it is really too weak for use. It is inadvisable to strengthen by adding nitrate of silver, for although it may be classed as chemically pure it may not be *photographically* pure. The best plan is to make up a strong solution of silver, say 100 to 150 grains per oz., make *slightly* alkaline with pure ammonia and expose to sunlight for a few days, then filter; this solution can then be used to strengthen weak but otherwise good baths without fear of putting them out of order.

The **developer** used is as follows :—

Iron protosulphate	250 gms.
Glacial acetic acid	150 c. c.
Water	3,000 c. c.
Alcohol	150 c. c.
Gelatine	5 gms.

An old bath becomes charged with solvents from the collodion, and a sufficient quantity of spirits of wine is then required to allow the developer to flow evenly and readily over the film. Very little is required when the bath is new.

An excess of developer washing over the edges of the glass carries with it some of the free nitrate of silver and causes the negative to lack density. A greater amount of density is obtained by the addition of gelatine, and 50 gms. dissolved in a few ounces of water and added to 3 litres of glacial acetic acid and kept as a stock solution has given good results. Scum which forms on a glass may be due to a deficiency of acetic acid in the developer, or to under-exposure and prolonged development.

Fixing—

Soda hyposulphite ...	No figures need be given for fixing baths, but the most satisfactory strength is found to be 4 ozs. hypo to 20 B. of water.
Water	

Stains arise through incomplete fixation, either through the continued use of a weak bath, or by rushing the glasses through and not allowing sufficient time for the silver iodide to disappear.

It is a good plan to leave the glass in the bath for a few seconds after the disappearance of the silver iodide. Perfect fixation and washing must always be given, or fading and stains will inevitably result.

Intensifying—

Sulphate of copper ...	...	240 gms.
Potassium bromide ...	...	120 ,,
Water ...	...	3,000 c. c.

A little fresh solution is added each morning, and the bath is entirely renewed every three days. This is followed by—

Silver nitrate	...	50 gms.
Nitric acid	...	10 c. c.
Water ...	...	1,000 c. c.

This solution is kept at the proper strength by adding silver when necessary. It is filtered occasionally.

Negatives of engraved sheets and plain negatives from hill-shade originals are bleached as usual with the copper sulphate solution and blackened with following :—

Hydroquinone ...	...	$\frac{1}{2}$ oz.
Sodium sulphite	...	1 ,,
Ammonia ...	...	$\frac{1}{4}$,,
Water ...	...	4 ,,

After the negative has been fixed and washed, it is bleached in the bromide of copper solution, quickly washed and placed in the silver solution to blacken. This increases the amount of deposit by precipitating more silver. As a yet further increase of density is necessary when making a negative of a black and white drawing, this operation is repeated, when a considerable increase in opacity is produced.

The negative is then washed, rinsed with a weak solution of nitric acid (1 in 100), washed again and carefully examined. If the bath is in good working order and the exposure, &c., correct, the deposit should be intensely black, and the lines clear and bright, and free from all deposit. If there is any slight deposit on the lines, the negative may be treated with the following clearing solutions.

Iodine clearing solutions.

Iodine ...	...	...	10 gms.
Potassium iodide	...	...	20 ,,
Water ...	...	...	3,000 c. c.

or

Potassium cyanide	...	...	15 gms.
Water ...	...	...	600 c. c.

Take sufficient iodine solution and flow it over the negative for about half a minute, then wash under the tap and apply the cyanide; this should clear away the veil, but if not, the operation may be repeated; if necessary put the negative through the intensifying baths a third time. This will do for a negative that is not required to be kept for any length of time and is wanted for rough work only, but the operation of clearing and dosing important negatives three times with bromide of copper and sliver is not recommended.

Powder Section.

Sensitising solution—

Glucose, liquid	...	...	$\frac{1}{2}$ oz.
Gelatine	...	...	60 grains.
Gum arabic	...	...	120 ,,
Amonium bichromate	...	...	$\frac{1}{2}$ oz.
Water	...	...	8 ,,

Glycerine, as necessary; depending on humidity of the atmosphere.

The gum and geletine are soaked in the water until soft; the other ingredients are added, and the whole warmed and strained. Until dry, it is insensitive to light.

Apply the solution with a sponge, or by pouring a little, on the glass. Level it with a soft India-rubber roller, until "tacky." Finish the drying in a warm box, away from all light.

After exposure, allow the film to take up moisture, in the drakened room, for a few minutes; then put it film upwards on the developing box. Rub gentle with a pad of English cotton wool and lamp black.

Retouching Section.

Varnish for negatives.

Gum dammar	...	...	200 gms.
Gum myrrh	...	...	50 ,,
Benzole	...	...	5 litres

The amount of benzole varies with the quality of the dammar resin.

Duffing medium—

Indian ink	... ...	16 cakes.
Carbolic acid	... ...	1 oz.
Decoction of ox-galls	...	½ oz.
Water	... up to ...	80 ozs.

or, the preparation known as Photopake. To prevent its being attacked by insects or cracking after use on the negative it is mixed in the following proportions.

Photopake	... ...	20 ozs.
Carbolic acid	... ..	1 oz.
Glycerine	... ...	½ oz.

Helio. Section.

Cleaning bath for zinc plates—

Alum	... ...	500 gms.
Nitric acid	... ...	100 c. c.
Water	... ...	6,000 c. c.

With perfectly grained, fresh zinc plates the cleaning bath should not be necessary. It is however a safeguard and is not found to affect the printing qualities of the plate.

Sensitising solution—

Dry egg albumen	... ...	5 oz.
Ammonium bichromate	...	2 ,,
Potassium bichromate	...	1 ,,
Water	...	100—120 ,,
Ammonium carbonate	...	2 ,,
Alcohol	... ...	2 ,,

To make up this solution, switch up the albumen in half the quantity of water and allow it to stand over night. Dissolve the salts in the remainder of the water and add to the dissolved albumen; then add the alcohol gradually and filter the whole thoroughly.

The plate as received from the graining shed is placed on a flat board and scrubbed under running water with a piece of soft felt. It is then thoroughly rinsed and while wet is coated with the sensitising solution. The first quantity of solution is allowed to drain into the sink and a second quantity applied. The plate is then, without draining, placed on a rotating whirler and slowly revolved over a series of gas jets. The greatest care must be taken that the plate is not allowed to become too warm, a heat which can be comfortably borne by the back of the hand being the greatest permissible. Immediately the plate shows signs of drying, the gas is extinguished and the drying completed by the blast from an electric fan. Exposure is made as soon as possible after the plate is dry, as the albumen film rapidly becomes insoluble, especially in damp weather.

After exposure the plate is laid on a sheet of paper and evenly and thinly coated with the ink solution. This is done by means of cloth pads. When the solvents have evaporated, the plate is soaked in water and developed.

Sponges are used for the preliminary development, and cotton wool for finishing.

Helio. Ink—

Winstone's special zinco. ink	...	2 oz.
Turpentine	... ...	1,000 c. c.
Benzole	... ...	500 c. c.

The ink used is very important, and the above has been found to give the best results.

Vandyke Section.

Sensitiser—

China glue (bazar) ...	...	1 oz.
Ammonium bichromate	...	50 grains.
Frankfort black ...	...	50 ,,
Water ...	...	4 oz.

For thick originals 100 grains of bichromate are used in lieu of 50.

The plate is coated with a soft sponge or roller. The Frankfort black allows the operator to see when the film is even.

Ink—

1	{ Lithographic writing ink	...	4 sticks (4 oz.)
	{ Burgundy pitch	...	...	8 oz.
	{ Turpentine	...	...	20 ,,
2	{ Bitumen	...	...	16 oz
	{ Benzole	...	...	10 ,,
	{ Turpentine	...	...	20 ,,
3	{ Special zinco. ink ...	...	16 oz.
	{ Lucca oil	...	...	2 ,,

Black lead powder—

Black lead	...	...	100 grains.
French chalk (talc) ...		...	100 ,,

Developer—

Hot water followed by—

Hydrochloric acid	...	...	20 c. c.
Water	...	..	1,000 ,,

Process Engraving Section.

COLOUR SENSITISERS—

Red sensitiser—

Pinacyanol	...	...	5 gms.
Alcohol	...	...	1,000 c. c.

10 c.c. of this solution is added to 300 c.c. of collodion emulsion or is diluted with distilled water, and used as a bath for gelatine dry plates. In either case the plate must be very well washed before exposure.

Green sensitiser—

Picric acid	...	...	1 gm.
Erythrosin	...	...	1 ,,
Silver nitrate	...	...	1 ..
Alcohol	...	...	1,000 c. c.

The silver is dissolved in the smallest possible quantity of water, and ammonia added drop by drop, till the precipitate first formed is dissolved. It is then added to the alcoholic erythrosin solution and filtered through paper. This sensitiser is flowed over a collodion emulsion plate, or is diluted with water and used to bathe gelatine dry plates. The plates are not washed before exposure.

These sensitisers are most useful when monochrome reproductions of coloured or badly stained originals are required. The sensitiser and absorption of the colour filter used depend on the colours of the subject, and the result required.

Sensitiser for carbon tissue.

Potassium bichromate	...	3 oz.
Potassium carbonate	...	1 ,,
Alcohol	...	10 ,,
Water	...	10 ,,

The proportion of alcohol is increased in damp hot weather.

Enamel for half-tone and copper and zinc etching.

Fish glue (Lepage's or Chanticleer) ...	6 oz.
Fluid egg albumen	4 ,,
Ammonium bichromate (Merk's) ...	180 grains.
Ammonia 880°	10 drops.
Water	10 oz.

The albumen is measured, well switched, and dissolved with the glue in half the quantity of water. The bichromate is dissolved in the other half, and the two mixed. The ammonia is then added and the whole well switched, and allowed to stand for twelve hours. It is then carefully filtered through cotton wool.

The following formula is also found to work well.

China glue	5 oz.
Water	5 ,,
Ammonium bichromate ...	160 grains.
Green citrate of iron and ammonia	5 ,,
Chrome Alum	5 ,,
Glucose	20 ,,
Water	5 oz.
Fluid egg albumen	4 ,,

Clearing bath for copper etching.

Glacial acetic acid	250 c. c.
Water	250 c. c.
Sodium chloride	50 gms.

Etching bath for half-tone.

Solution of perchloride of iron in water to register 35° Beaumé. This is toned down by adding one-fourth of an old bath.

Cyanotype Process.

Stock solutions—

Green citrate of iron and ammonia	25 gms.
Water	100 c. c.
Potassium ferricyanide ...	25 gms.
Water	100 c. c.

For use mix in equal proportions.

The stock solutions keep well, but the mixed solution must be carefully protected from light and used up at once.

Special Litho. or Hollingworth paper can be used. The former gives the best result.

No clearing bath required.

Chocolate Prints.

A {
Silver nitrate ... ... 30 gms.
Water ... ... 100 c. c.
Ammonia 880° ... ... sufficient.

B {
Green citrate of iron and ammonia ... 50 gms.
Water ... ... 100 c. c.

Use two parts A to one of B ; add A to B.

Appendix II.

FORMULÆ FOR LITHOGRAPHIC DEPARTMENT.

1. Old work is cleaned off zinc with caustic potash, the plate being subsequently mopped over with a solution of sulphuric acid.

The plate is then polished with snakestone, after which it is put on the graining machine for 40 minutes.

2. ETCHING SOLUTION—

1 lb. of gall nuts, bruised, and soaked for 24 hours in a gallon of water, and boiled down to half its bulk; when cool a little borax is added. For use, take equal parts of the above, and of fresh gum solution, and slightly acidify with phosphoric acid.

3. GUM SOLUTION—

Boiling water   ...   ...   9 pints.
Pure gum arabic   ...   ...   3 lbs.

The gum is soaked, boiled, and strained. It is essential that it should be fresh every day.

4. TRANSFER PAPER—

(a) Transparent—

Before coating, the tissue paper is treated on both sides with copal varnish 1 pint and turpentine $\frac{1}{2}$ pint.

(b) Copper plate transfer paper—

Plaster of Paris   ...   ...   1 lb.
Flour paste   ...   ... $\frac{1}{2}$,,

The plaster should be continually stirred, and water added a little at a time as it tends to set, until all setting power is lost; it is then mixed with the flour paste. The paper should be coated twice.

(c) Ordinary transfer paper—

Gamboge	...	...	...	½ ℔.
Water	...	...	...	10 ozs.
Arrowroot	...	...	...	½ ℔.
Water	...	...	...	10 ozs.

The gamboge is soaked and boiled, and added to the boiled arrowroot. Before being coated, the paper is first sized with a mixture of 1 oz. of isinglass to 15 ozs. of water.

Sensitising a zinc plate or stone for corrections.

One in 60 of citric acid.

5. ETCHING HELIO. PLATES—

The plate is inked in, dried, and dusted with finely powdered resin, well washed to remove the resin from the grain of the plate, dried, and well rubbed with a pad of cotton wool charged with Russell's powder until the work has a decided polish.

It is then etched, in a weak solution of nitric acid (1 in 80). This etching leaves the work slightly in relief, and must not be confused with the ordinary etching solution previously described. This second etching is not usually necessary. Plates etched in this manner must be re-polished before they can again be used for any fresh work.

6. THE PREPARATION OF A SET-OFF—

It is found that Double Imperial, 40lbs., bank post paper, when treated on both sides with copal varnish 1 pint, turpentine ½ pint, retains its shape and size very well.

A set-off from a helio. is prepared by pulling an impression either on paper varnished as above or on a polished zinc plate according to the purpose for which it is required.

This impression is then dusted with magnesia and Frankfort black and, then transferred either to a helio or to a clean zinc plate as may necessary.

Appendix III.

NOTES ON THE USE OF VARYING METHODS OF DEVELOPMENT AND INTENSIFICATION OF NEGATIVES.

The difficulty of retaining the very finest lines of a drawing and at the same time keeping the heavy work open and clear is well known. Theoretically a line should reproduce exactly in proportion to the amount of reduction, but this is not so in practice, owing to the "spreading" action which takes place during (a) Exposure, (b) Development, and (c) Intensification.

(a) By irradiation or scattering of light in the film during exposure, (this should be distinguished from "halation" which is due to light passing through the film and being reflected back on to the film from the glass, and rarely occurs with wet collodion).

The problem of overcoming irradiation has never been satisfactorily solved; some experimental work has been done in the Photo.-Litho. Office and promising results obtained by the use of picric acid.

(b) Spreading action during development, owing to the fact that the particles of silver haloid acted on by light, have, during development, the property of reducing or acting on adjoining particles which have not been exposed to light; this was proved by Abney, and is easily and conclusively demonstrated.

(c) Spreading action during intensification. This is unavoidable when great density is required, as for helio. work.

As the spreading or closing action during intensification is almost directly proportional to the density given by any particular formula, this can be remedied to a certain extent by varying the exposure.

Bearing in mind the difficulties explained above, eleven negatives were taken and intensified with the various formulæ given in the tabulated statement below:—

When using lead ferricyanide and sodium sulphide, and mercury bichloride and ammonia, which are the two extremes of the formulæ given in the table, the exposure is as 1 to 4, the other formulæ occupying an intermediate place as regards density and exposure.

Appendices.

	Bleached with.	Blackened with	
No. 1	Lead ferricyanide	Sodium sulphide	
No. 2	Mercury bichloride	Ammonia	
No. 3	Copper bromide	Silver nitrate	Repeated.
No. 4	Redevelopment & mercury bichloride.	Ammonia	
No. 5	Mercuric iodide	Sodium sulphide	
No. 6	Copper bromide	Schlippes salt	
No. 7	Copper bromide	Silver nitrate followed by sodium sulphide.	
No. 8	Copper bromide	Silver nitrate followed by iodine & Schlippes salt.	
No. 9	Mercury bichloride	Sodium sulphide.	
No. 10	Copper bromide	Silver nitrate followed by potassium ferricyanide & sodium sulphide.	
No. 11	Redevelopment & mercuric iodide.	Sodium sulphide.	

No. 3 though not quite so good as No. 2 is the formula in general use on account of its reliability, freedom from stain and its lasting qualities. No. 2 though producing excellent results is unreliable, and the negative fades after a time; it and 4 are used occasionally while No. 7 is employed for the preparation of half-tone and line blocks. Nos. 5 and 6 are unreliable.

These experiments form a record, and are the outcome of many previous similar experiments carried out in the Photo.-Litho. Office by Mr. R. Taylor, lately Photo. Manager. An inspection of the results is gratifying, as it proves that the formula as at present used is the best all round method for the work of the office.

The experience of the Photo.-Litho. Office since 1908 tends to show that the best results are obtained when the originals are drawn for reduction by one-half; one-third reduction also gives good results, but by a greater or less reduction than these the results are inferior.

Appendix IV.
NOTES ON THE HELIO. PROCESS.

In any note on the Helio Process the first item that presents itself for examination is the graining of the plates.

The best photographic results are obtained on polished zinc, but a "grain" is necessary for printing purposes to enable the plate to carry sufficient water, to prevent the ink "catching" during the return passage under the machine rollers. As the photographic and printing requirements are thus diametrically opposed to each other, many experiments have been made from time to time to get a grain suitable for both. The moisture-carrying capacity of a plate does not depend on the actual roughness of the grain, but on the sharpness of it. A plate grained with a very hard sand or emery may be smoother in surface than one grained with soft sand, yet have much better printing qualities. In England, pumice powder used with glass, china, or wooden balls is commonly used, but in Calcutta it has been found that zinc balls and sharp fresh water sand gives the best results.

Pumice powder has been tried, but although the plates were excellent for the photographic part of the work and passed the proving stage satisfactorily, they gave great trouble in the machine.

The grain was too smooth and could not carry sufficient water to prevent the ink "catching." Plates grained thus were used for a short time and then abandoned.

Hooghly river sand, obtained near Calcutta has been found to answer the purpose well.

The graining of the plates being considered, we turn to the sensitising solution.

The helio or direct photo-zinco process (as distinguished from the transfer process) was first introduced in the Survey of India by Sergt. J. Harrold, R.E.

His process was as follows :—

The plate was desensitised* with a solution of gallic and phosphoric acid and gum arabic, then coated with bichromated albumen, exposed under a negative, developed in water and dried, after which it was coated with a thin film of litho. printing ink by means of a lithographic roller.

On sprinkling the plate with water and continuing the rolling the image gradually clears up, leaving an image composed of light-hardened albumen coated with a more or less greasy ink.

*i. e rendered insensitive to grease.

The fatal defect of this process was that as the zinc was desensitised before coating, the image was only retained on the plate by the mechanical adhesion of the light-hardened albumen.

This meant that any abrasion, friction or absorption of water by the albumen image during printing would spoil the plate.

Latterly the process was modified by inking up after exposure and before development. This simplified the work but did not get over the defect caused by the previous desensitising. The true case of this defect was not understood, and was attributed to decomposition of the albumen film owing to the moist heat of Bengal. Acting on this supposition experiments were made to obtain a process by which the ink image would be in direct contact with the metal, with no intervening layer of albumen or other colloid. The result of these experiments was Mr. Turner's "ink" process. In this process the *desensitised* zinc plate was coated by means of a sponge with a thin film composed of —

> Transfer ink
> Fish glue
> Soap
> Ammonium bichromate.

The plate was then exposed under the negative and developed in water. This process had the same defect as the previous one and several of its own. The ink process was in use up to the end of 1905. In January 1906 the use of fish glue in the albumen solution, and the preliminary desensitising of the plates which was the cause of all the previous trouble were abandoned, and since then the albumen process has been exclusively used.

The formula at present in use is that on page 36.

Dry egg albumen is used because it is much more reliable than fluid albumen and is also cheaper in use.

The mixture of potassium and ammonium bichromate is designed to give the greatest possible ink-holding capacity to the film. It is a fact well known to collotype workers that a plate sensitised with ammonium bichromate alone is liable to give glazed shadows, which take ink with difficulty or not at all. This tendency is counteracted by the addition of potassium bichromate.

Ammonium carbonate is used to increase the solubility of the albumen and at the same time to improve the keeping qualities of the coated plates. Liq. ammonia serves the same purpose, but being more volatile is less permanent in its action.

A small quantity of alcohol reduces the tendency for air bubbles to form when coating the plate.

The formula has been varied and improved from time to time through continued experiment.

The potassium bichromate was added some seven years ago and the ammonium carbonate substituted for liq. ammonia in 1913.

We now turn to the printing of the helio from the negative.

To obtain the best possible helio, it is essential that the zinc plate should be in absolute contact with the negative. This contact is obtained as far as possible with the aid of the pneumatic printing frame, but observation will at once make it apparent that this contact is not absolute, because of the thickness of the duffing medium on the negative. The duffing medium is laid on the negative as lightly as is consistent with its purpose, but a certain thickness is unavoidable; the effect being that the resultant want of absolute contact between the negative and the zinc plate permits diffused light to enter at the edges of the lines and produce a thickened line on the helio.

To obviate this difficulty in the making of half-tone helios, the helio is printed with the aid of a mirror which reflects the rays of the sun on to the negative in the printing frame, which is placed in shade and at exact right angles to the path of the reflected beam; and as a possible solution of the difficulty it was decided in 1914 to try this method for printing ordinary helios.

A tint negative was prepared from a half-tone screen and helios printed therefrom, one in the ordinary manner by direct sunlight, and the other with the aid of the mirror.

The printed results of the latter showed a very marked superiority over the former. These were considered so satisfactory and of such interest that orders were issued to print Degree Sheet 38 P and Standard Sheet 83 $\frac{B}{2}$ by both the old and the new methods. The improvement was equally pleasing. Helios prepared by the new method are found to be easier to print from than those by the old.

Ink can be laid on stronger and there is far less tendency for work to thicken and bung up on the plate.

The ink used in making a helio. is nearly if not quite as important as the sensitising solution, and must have the following properties :—

       (a) It should form a perfect resist to the etching or desensitising solution used by the lithographic printer.

(*b*) It should contain the greatest possible amount of colouring matter, for the reason that the best results are obtained when the film of ink is used extremely thin ; which means that if the colouring matter is too weak the lines appear grey, and on the grey surface of the zinc plate are difficult to see during development and final examination.

(*c*) It should adhere tenaciously to the light-hardened albumen and at the same time show no tendency to smear.

Formerly, the opinion was held that a helio ink should contain a considerable proportion of greasy matter, such as wax, stearine soap, &c. This idea is now exploded, as better results are obtained by using a simple solution of the best quality lithographic chalk ink. The ink is dissolved in a mixture of benzole and turpentine, and by varying the proportions of these two solvents, the ink can be made to conform to any required condition, climatic or otherwise. Lavender oil is added to prevent the ink oxidising or drying too quickly on the finished helio, and serves that purpose well without interfering with the working qualities of the ink.

The development requires a thoroughly practised hand and eye, and a good light.

Appendix V.

NOTES ON THE VANDYKE PROCESS.

The best original for the process is a perfectly drawn tracing on blue tracing cloth. Perfectly drawn means that *every line must be absolutely black and opaque:* a good test is to hold the tracing up against a very strong light and carefully examine it for any sign of greyness or transparency in the lines. If found grey or broken it should be returned to the draughtsman for re-inking. Drawings on paper will also give good results. A smooth wove paper preferably of a bluish shade should be used. Even more care must be taken in drawing on paper, as owing to its greater opacity the lines will look blacker than they really are. Yellow tracing paper or cloth is quite unsuitable and should never be used.

A good quality Indian ink freshly made up should be used. When drawing on tracing cloth a slight addition of ox-gall will make the ink "take" better. Heavy block letters or border lines may be gone over, twice, using "Photopake" the second time.

There are six operations in producing a printing plate, *viz.:*—

1.—Graining.	4.—1st Development.
2.—Sensitising.	5.—Inking.
3.—Exposing.	6.—2nd Development.

The graining having been completed, the plate should appear perfectly smooth with an even matt surface.*

The plate is then thoroughly well washed, back and front, the surplus water squeegeed off, and the plate quickly dried by heat. This is very important; otherwise the surface becomes oxidised and will give trouble in the after processes.

No pains should be spared to get perfectly grained plates, as the success of the work depends on that.

The plate is then sensitised with the solution given in Appendix I.

Break or cut the glue into small pieces and soak in 3 oz. of water till swelled and soft, then dissolve in a water bath; an open stove may be used but great care is required to prevent "burning". The glue being dissolved add the bichromate in fine powder, and stir till dissolved. The Frankfort black is then well ground in 1 oz. of water and added to the solution, and the whole thoroughly mixed and strained through fine cloth.

* See page 46.

The room used for coating the zinc plates should be illuminated by yellow light; either yellow glass windows or ordinary windows covered with two thicknesses of deep yellow cloth will suffice. It is not necessary but preferable to make up the solution in the coating room. Place the clean zinc plate on a sheet of paper a few inches larger than the plate, and coat by means of a soft sponge. Two sponges should be used, one for giving the preliminary coat and the other for finishing off.

The coating should not be thick and should show no bad streaks. A good deal of knack is required to do this quickly and successfully. When using the finishing sponge the strokes should be given the long way of the plate, finishing by two the short way one across each end. A better plan is to use an India-rubber roller.

The plate is then dried by heat and should not be made hotter than can be comfortably borne by the back of the hand. If this heat is exceeded the plate will be spoilt.

All operations from the coating of the plate to the 1st development must be done in a yellow-lighted room, and great care should be taken that no daylight reaches the plate.

Exposure.—The tracing to be copied is placed in the printing frame and the sensitised plate on top, the backing put in place and securely locked up. For sizes up to $36'' \times 24''$ the ordinary box pattern printing frame will give good contact, but for anything larger a pneumatic frame is necessary. Whichever pattern is used, care must be taken that the plate and tracing are in perfect contact, otherwise good results are impossible.

Direct sunlight is best for exposure and no fixed time can be given. A few trials will indicate the correct exposure. Length of exposure and class of original should be noted with a view to obtaining a correct scale of exposures for each class of original.

1st Development.—The exposure being complete the frame is taken into the yellow-lighted room, and the plate removed to a sink and well washed in running water. If the exposure has been correct, the lines of the drawing will develop out as sharp lines of clean zinc. Over exposure is denoted by the lines refusing to develop, or, where the exposure is only slightly in excess, by a slight scum on the lines; this can sometimes be remedied by gently passing a piece of soft cotton wool over the plate under running water, but it requires a light hand.

Under exposure is shown by the lines developing up thick and open, and the ground breaking away in spots or patches. If the exposure has been much deficient the whole film will wash off the plate. The development being finished, the plate is drained for a few seconds and is then blotted off with smooth sheets of clean blotting paper, which should not be rubbed but only patted : this prevents the wet paper being damaged and it can be dried and used over and over again. The plate being thoroughly blotted off is then dried, and all defects such as spots, scratches on the film, finger marks, &c., &c., gummed out with a thin solution of gum arabic ; a small quantity of aniline violet should be added to the gum to make the touching up visible. The edges of the plate and large patches of ground with no work can be gummed in by a small sponge. For smaller parts and working close to lines or lettering a fine sable hair brush should be used.

The gumming out finished, the plate is dried and is then ready for inking up.

The ink, the formula for which is given on page 36 is made up as follows :—

Melt the burgundy pitch and then add the sticks of litho. writing ink, stirring till all is dissolved. Remove from the fire and away from lights, and add 500. c. c. of turpentine, a little at a time, stirring well.

Grind the bitumen to a fine powder and put in another dish, add the benzole, let it stand for a few hours stirring occasionally till all the bitumen is dissolved, then add the remaining 500. c. c. turpentine.

The special zinco. ink is put in a small iron pot with two oz. lucca oil, and the oil and ink mixed by the aid of gentle heat and stirring ; this is a slow job and must be carefully done as the ink is easily burned. When the zinco. ink and oil have been mixed, a little of No. 2 is added and again well-mixed ; by gradually adding No. 2 the whole can be got into solution. When solution is complete No. 1 is then added and if the mixing has been properly done the ink should be of a smooth oily consistency and free from lumps of any kind. The ink is now strained through a cloth to remove any insoluble particles, and will keep indefinitely in a wide-mouthed stoppered bottle. The solution should always be well stirred up and vigorously shaken before taking out a supply for the day's work, since the ingredients are inclined to separate after standing for some time.

The zinc plate to be inked up is laid on a sheet of paper and a little of the ink solution poured on the centre and then spread evenly and thinly over the plate by means of a cloth pad ; if the ink is too thick to do this comfortably it may be thinned by adding a little of—

Turpentine ... 4 parts.
Benzole ... 1 part.

After inking up, the plates are put out in the sunlight for a few hours to dry thoroughly.

After drying, the following powder is well rubbed into the ink with a soft cloth :—

Powdered French chalk   ... 1 part.

Powdered black lead   ... 1 part.

2nd Development.—Immerse the plate in hot water for from 15 to 30 minutes and then put under running water, and develop with a soft sponge or a plug of cotton wool.

When development is nearly complete the plate is immersed for about 1 minute in a 1—500 solution of hydrochloric acid, then well washed, and the final cleaning completed with water and carbonate of magnesia : all spots, dirt, &c., are removed by using the magnesia powder with a pointed stick or a piece of felt. The plate is finally rinsed and wiped with a clean cloth and hung up to dry. When dry it is ready for the printer.

Appendix VI.

MEMORANDUM EXPLANATORY OF THE SCHEME OF REORGANISATION OF THE PHOTO.-LITHO. OFFICES AT CALCUTTA AND DEHRA DUN

(BY MAJOR W. C. HEDLEY, R.E., 1908).

At the request of the Surveyor General I have written a memorandum explanatory of the scheme of pay and promotion which I proposed and which was sanctioned by the Government of India in their letter No. 355-53-2 of 19th March 1908 and communicated to the A.S.G., P.L.O. by the Offg. Surveyor General in his letter No. 1058 of 25th March 1908. Copies of these letters are attached. The rules contained therein are very simple and require no explanation, but the success or failure of the new scheme will depend entirely on how it is worked, and I propose to take each section of the office in turn, to show how the pay and prospects of the men have been affected, and to explain the principles on which I consider the scheme should be worked.

FIRST DIVISION.

This division now consists of six* posts :—

Two of Rs. 500-25-750

Two of Rs. 350-10-500

Two of Rs. 250-10-400

The highest post in the past has been Rs. 500 as a maximum but Mr. Fogarty was specially engaged on a salary which rose to Rs. 550. Mr. Taylor, Mr. Oddy and Mr. Colquhoun were also engaged on special contracts and their pay does not represent posts fixed by the Government of India, but contracts arranged by the Secretary of State in England. It will probably be necessary in the future to obtain the services of men from England, and their pay will doubtless be settled by the Secretary of State, and will very possibly vary from the figures now laid down. Those figures can not however be departed from without the sanction of Government, and they represent the salaries for which it is thought that suitable men can be obtained.

---

* One of the posts is at present (1919) held by Dehra Dun.

The object of the first division is to provide technical skill of the first quality in the photographic and lithographic departments. It is to attract this skill that the pay has been so largely increased. The whole efficiency of the department depends on the necessary technical skill being obtained. By far the two most important posts are those of the Managers of the Photographic and Lithographic departments. If they are good men their departments will be good; if they are inefficient, their departments will assuredly be the same although it is always possible that their inefficiency may be partially atoned for by the skill of their subordinates. Of the other four posts one is intended for the Assistant Superintendent of the Photo. department and the other three for the Litho. department. The work of the latter is fairly described by the titles, "Foremen Litho. Printer", "Chief Machine Printer" and "Chief Prover". All these men are comparatively useless unless they are really 1st class men at their respective trades.

All the men now in the first division have been brought out from England. It would however be quite wrong to lay down a rule that the first division must always be recruited from England. It is a mistake to assume that because a man comes from England he is necessarily better than a man who happens to have been born in India. Some of the men we have had from England have been good and some bad. I look forward to the time when the standard of technical skill will be much higher than it is at present right through the office, and when it will be unnecessary to go to England to fill all the posts in the first division. If a man in the Second division is good enough he should be promoted to fill a vacancy in the first, but there must be no doubt about his qualifications, and promotion to the first division must be by selection and not by seniority. Seniority must have nothing whatever to say to it. Efficiency is the only test. The fact that a man holds one of the junior posts in the first division gives him no claims whatever to promotion to the higher posts. A man might be an admirable machine hand and be a failure as foreman litho. printer, and quite useless in charge of the Litho. Department. In the same way it by no mean follows that the Assistant Superintendent Photo. or the Foreman Litho. Printer will be promoted on a vacancy to the posts of the Superintendent, Photo. or Litho. He will probably be so promoted, because he will probably have been selected for the second post with a view to advancement to the first. If however his abilities or qualifications are not such as to fit him for the higher post he has no claim whatever to it, and no grievance if he is not given it. This cannot be too clearly understood. In such a case it would probably be necessary to go to England, and secure the services of the best man who could be got.

I have said that technical skill is absolutely necessary for the men of the first division but this is not all that is required. The power of managing the men under them and of teaching them, the ability to organize work and get it done, and finally zeal and energy, are almost equally necessary.

SECOND DIVISION.

The second division has been nominally reduced in number from 22 to 17* but this reduction is more apparent than real, for four of the old posts were for apprentices only. The real reduction in number is from 18 to 17. It is hard not to use the word "posts", but to do so is to give an inaccurate description of the present state of affairs. The word at once conveys the idea that there will always be one man whose pay is fixed at each of the figures there laid down. That however is not the case. These figures are *maxima* beyond which the Surveyor General may not raise the pay, but it was never intended that the pay of all the men in the 2nd Division should be raised to those maxima. The rule now is that the Surveyor General may give any rate of pay *which he thinks a man deserves* provided that these maxima are not exceeded.

These *maxima* are—

One of Rs. 350.

Two of Rs. 300.

Two of Rs. 250.

Twelve of Rs. 200.

A man may be on any rate of pay the Surveyor General likes to fix from 100 to 350, but only one may be as high as Rs. 350, only two as high as Rs. 300, etc. If there is no man in the division worth Rs. 350 that pay will not be given; possibly there may only be one man worth 300, the next man may be sufficiently paid with Rs. 280 or Rs. 260 and so on. In the past men have occasionally been promoted from the third division to the 2nd, but the usual method of recruiting was to engage apprentices, who in due course received appointments in the 2nd division. In future the rule will be that the 2nd division will be recruited from the 3rd, but in exceptional cases it may be desirable to engage specially qualified men and put them straight into the 2nd division. This however will very seldom occur and the ordinary routine is that all men will start in the 3rd division and will work their way through it. The time they formerly spent as apprentices they will now spend in the 3rd division, but whereas their pay formerly rose by annual increments from 10 to 40 and then

---

* Two of the posts are at present (1919) held by Dehra Dun.

jumped to 100, their pay will now be fixed by the Surveyor General according to their merits. I shall presently explain in detail the rules governing promotion in the 3rd division but these rules will not hold for men who show by their zeal and ability that they are qualified or qualifying for the 2nd division. They should be specially promoted by suitable increments (say Rs. 10, 15, or 20 annually according to their ability) until their pay approximates to Rs. 100. Above that figure there cannot be more than 17 men at any one time, but as vacancies occur suitable men are promoted from the third to the 2nd division and then by suitable increments at suitable intervals to higher rates fo pay in the 2nd division.

It must be clearly understood by every man who is appointed to the second division that he has no claims whatever to have his pay increased to the maxima there laid down. His promotion to the second division means that in the opinion of the Surveyor General he is worth more than Rs. 100 per mensem. It by no means follows that he will ever be worth Rs. 250 or 350. The great root principle of the scheme is that the longer service a man has the more pay he should get (always assuming efficiency) but that his promotion should be rapid or slow in proportion to his ability. Thus in the second division a very good man might be rapidly promoted, say by annual increments of Rs. 10 or 15 to the highest available posts in the second division or even to the first; a less good but still good man might be promoted by biennial increments of Rs. 10, or annual increments of Rs. 5. He would probably never rise above Rs. 250. A fair man, who was, say, promoted to the 2nd divison at the age of 30 would probably never rise above Rs. 200 and his increments should be so allotted as to place him at that figure at about 50 years of age. Others again might never get beyond Rs. 150. The rate and extent of a man's promotion are entirely a matter of what he is worth.

It is a mistake to run a man too rapidly up to the maximum he is worth and then leave him without hope of promotion. It is better to promote him more slowly at first, and finally to push him a little beyond what he is actually worth. Every man works better if he still has chance of promotion.

It often happens that a man works well and gets into the second division and then becomes slack or indifferent. Under the old system he knew quite well that his promotion was a certainty. Under the new system his pay should not be increased and if necessary it should be reduced. It is here that the advantage of small and comparatively frequent increments comes in. The beneficial effect of the stoppage of an expected increment is often very great.

THIRD DIVISION.

The pay of the men in the new 3rd division, which combines the old 3rd and 4th divisions, is fixed by the Surveyor General subject to a maximum of Rs. 100 per mensem. Formerly no promotions could be made except to fill a vacancy caused by the death or retirement of one of the senior men. Now the Surveyor General can make any promotions* he pleases subject to the two conditions :—

1. That no man receives more than Rs. 100.

2. That the budget estimate for the year is not exceeded.

It is evident at once that some guiding rules are necessary to assist the Assistant Surveyor General, Photo.-Litho. Office in his recommendations and the Surveyor General in his decisions. Rules have been laid down and I will try and explain them.

The first thing to remember is the principle, to which I have already alluded in my remarks on the 2nd division, *viz.*, that the pay of every efficient man increases with his length of service but *the pace at which it increases is in proportion to the merits and abilities of the man.* No man should be retained in the department who does not do good work. Idle and inefficient men should be discharged. There will however always be a great difference in quality amongst those men who may be called efficient. Some will be very good and above the average, some will be average (and these will be the great majority) and some will be below the average. I have suggested, and the Surveyor General has approved, certain rates of pay which should ordinarily be paid to superior, average, and below average men at each period of their service. These rates vary for each trade. There are many trades, the skill required for each of which varies. The rate of pay laid down for each trade at each period of a man's service varies in accordance with the skill required. These rates are laid down for each year of service for superior, average, and below average men. The *maximum* rate laid down is of course Rs. 100 per mensem and this rate will only be paid to the best men towards the end of their service. It is not proposed to publish these rates but, for the sake of making this explanation clear, I will give an imaginary table for one trade ; we will take, say that of a carpenter.

---

* The number of " permanent " men in the 3rd Division, in Calcutta and Dehra combined, is limited to 100.

The table would be as follows :—

	Salary in rupees on joining	at 5 years service	at 10 years	at 15 years	at 20 years	at 25 years	at 30 years service
Carpenters Superior	10	30	45	60	75	85	100
Average	10	20	35	50	65	70	75
Below Average	10	16	28	35	40	45	50

A boy would usually join at about 15 years of age. He would know nothing, but he would be paid Rs. 10 in the hope of at tracting a good class of boy. In the course of a year or two it would become evident whether he was worth keeping or not. If he is not likely to prove useful he should be discharged as soon as it becomes clear that he will probably never be efficient. If he is retained as efficient his pay will in future be regulated by the table of pay. Working by this table he would at 5 years service receive Rs. 30 a month if he was very good, Rs. 20 if he was average, and Rs. 16 if he was distinctly below the average. Very possibly he would receive some intermediate rate of pay, *e.g.*, Rs. 25 if he was very good but not the very best, or Rs. 18 if he was only slightly below the average. His average annual rate of advancement would be approximately Rs. 3 if he was superior, Rs. 2 if he was average, and Rs. 1-8-0 if he was below the average. His rate of advancement would depend entirely on himself. The promotion of one man would in no way involve the keeping back of another.

The table of pay here given is purely imaginary and is only to exemplify the system, but tables of pay have been laid down for every trade in the Photo.-Litho. Office and promotions will be given in accordance with the rates laid down in those tables. These rates are entirely at the discretion of the Surveyor General and may be changed by him from time to time.

The *maxima* are not of course as high as Rs. 100 for every trade. The rates for each trade have been carefully considered and vary in proportion to the skill required and to the value of the work performed.

Increase of pay are sanctioned by the Surveyor General on the recommendation of the Assistant Surveyor General, Photo.-Litho. Office, forwarded through the Director of Map Publication. These recommendations are prepared on the prescribed forms and reach the Surveyor General twice a year, during the months of May and November so that, if approved, the increases may take effect from the first day of those months. The average rate of increase is evident from the tables, but it is a rule that no man may receive an increase more than once a year without the special sanction of the Surveyor General. It is not necessary therefore to consider the cases of those men who have received an increase of pay within the year, but those who have had an increase on, say May 1st 1908 should again have their claims considered on May 1st 1909. Only the names of those whom the Assistant Surveyor General considers worthy of promotion should be forwarded to the Surveyor General.

It would appear at first sight that these annual increases would result in enlarged budgets, but the remedy is of course that savings are continually being provided by the death or retirement of the older men. Under the old system the retirement of a senior man on, say, Rs. 100 meant promotion to all those underneath him. Under the new system it merely means that Rs. 100 per mensem are available for providing increases of pay for other men. These increases are not to be given at once. They must wait till the next 1st May or 1st November as the case may be, when the claims and merits of all the employés will be duly considered*.

It is not until all the employés are paid at the proper rates that the increases will on the average be balanced by the savings due to retirements. For the next few years it is probable that the increments which ought to be given will considerably exceed the savings due to retirements. The reason of this is that many of the staff have up to the present been underpaid. Before the budget estimate for any one year is sent in, a rough calculation must be made of the increases it is proposed to give, and of the savings from which these increases can be met. If the savings are not sufficient an increased budget allotment must be asked for. I pointed out when I first proposed the scheme that an increased budget allotment might ultimately be necessary.

Under the new rules there is no fixed number of posts.— The Surveyor General can increase the staff by engaging new hands, or decrease it by not filling vacancies, or by discharging those men who are not yet on the permanent list. It is probable that as the staff becomes more efficient fewer men will be required. This means that

* *NOTE.—Since 1909, promotions have taken place annually, with effect from the 1st April.*

more money will be available in the way of savings for increasing the pay of those employés who have become more efficient. For instance, suppose that 3 coolies on Rs. 8 a month had been in the habit of coating 15 negatives a day and one of the coolies left. If the other two proved able to do the same amount of work as was formerly done by three, they undoubtedly deserve more pay. The same principle would apply throughout the office. There is no doubt that a comparatively small staff, well paid, contented and fully employed does better work than a large staff which has much of its time idle.

THE INFERIOR ESTABLISHMENT.

The Surveyor General has full power to regulate the staff of the inferior establishment as he pleases. Men on this establishment are for the most part unskilled, or possess only a very small modicum of skill. They are mostly coolies and do not belong to any recognized trade. They would include men graining plates, coating negatives, covering rollers, press assistants, machine feeders, etc., etc. It is not possible or necessary to lay down tables of pay for men of this class, but their pay should be periodically considered and revised by the Assistant Surveyor General, and any man who is able and willing to do a good day's work should be paid a living wage and not a dole of Rs. 5 per mensem, as many of them are at present. At the present moment the working hours are short and many of the men are inefficient and do very little work, and I feel sure that, in this division especially, the numbers can be largely decreased, and the efficiency increased at the same time. If this is done the pay of the remaining efficient men should undoubtedly be increased. I have said that this division should include press assistants, but I am aware that many men who are only press assistants were already in the old 4th division when this scheme was sanctioned, and have accordingly become part of the new 3rd division. In future no man should be put into that division unless he is being trained to a trade, and if he shows no promise or aptitude he should be removed from the 3rd division and either discharged, or relegated to the inferior establishment. There is no reason why men in the inferior establishment should not be promoted to the 3rd division, if they show that they are likely to become efficient at a trade.

In conclusion I wish to point out the immense power of selection which this system gives to the Assistant Surveyor General and his superintendents. The best men can be pushed on, the inferior men can be kept back. Idle and inefficient men can be discharged until they get a pensionable post, *i.e.*, until they have from 10 to 15 years service. It can not be too strongly stated that young men should be discharged if they are idle, or if they show no aptitude for the work. Nothing spoils an office so much as the retention of young and worthless men. It is not too much to say that the Assistant Surveyor General and his superintendents are now provided with every facility for making their staff efficient, and it will be their own fault if it does not become so. I also wish to point out what an excellent opportunity is now offered to a young man joining the office and wishing to get on. It rests entirely with himself whether he advances slowly or rapidly, and although only a comparatively small proportion can rise to the 2nd division, yet the best will always rise.

W. C. HEDLEY, *Major, R.E.*

Calcutta,
May 23rd, 1908.

Copy of letter No. 355-53-2, dated Calcutta, the 19th March 1908, from the Secretary to the Government of India, Department of Revenue and Agriculture (Land Surveys), to the Surveyor General of India.

With reference to your letter No. 584, dated the 21st February last, I am directed to communicate the following orders of the Government of India on the scheme for the reorganisation of the Photo.-Lithographic Offices of the Survey of India.

2. It has been proposed that the First Division, which at present comprises seven appointments, should in future consist of only six men who should draw pay to be fixed by the Surveyor General subject to certain maxima and minima rates. The Government of India approve of the reduction proposed in the number of appointments, but they think it would be more satisfactory to give incremental pay so fixed that a man whose work was satisfactory would rise to the maximum in fifteen years. It would of course be open to the Surveyor General to stop any increment if dissatisfied with the man's work or conduct. I am accordingly to convey the sanction of the Government of India to the constitution of the First Division as follows :—

> Two appointments on Rs. 500-25-750.
> Two appointments on Rs. 350-10-500.
> Two appointments on Rs. 250-10-400.

All these posts will be pensionable.

3. As regards the Second Division which at present consists of 22 men on fixed pay, the proposal that the number of posts should be reduced to seventeen is accepted. For the seventeen posts the maximum pay will be fixed as follows :—

One post ...	...	...	Rs. 350.
Two posts ...	...	...	Rs. 300.
Two posts ...	...	...	Rs. 250.
Twelve posts	...	...	Rs. 200.

The Surveyor General may give any rate of pay which he thinks each man deserves provided that these maxima are not exceeded. All these posts will be pensionable.

4. The following arrangements are sanctioned in connection with the Third and Fourth Division —

(1) There will be no fixed number of appointments and no fixed rates of pay. The Surveyor General may increase or reduce the number of men employed from time to time, and raise or lower the pay of each man subject to the following conditions :—

(a) The total cost of the present Third and Fourth Division together must be met from the budget grant for the year.

(b) No man must be paid more than Rs. 100 a month without the sanction of the Government of India.

(2) Each individual man, who at present holds a permanent pensionable post, will continue to have his claim to pension under the general rules; but all new hands will be brought in on a temporary footing until the total number of men having a claim to pension is reduced by retirement or death to 100. Thereafter the number of men having a claim to pension must not at any time exceed 100. Subject to this condition the Surveyor General may declare any man to have a claim to pension, provided he has rendered at least 10 years approved service on a temporary footing, in which case his previous continuous temporary service will count towards pension.

5. With reference to the inferior establishment the Surveyor General is authorised to excercise full powers as regards the numbers, the rates of pay, the appointment and dismissal of the staff and may also grant a claim to pension to any man who has rendered ten years approved service.

6. The Surveyor General is also authorised to transfer savings under one head of the sanctioned budget estimates of the Photo.-Litho. Office to expenditure under another head in the same office.

7. I am to add that the Government of India sanction the introduction of this scheme with effect from the 1st April 1908.

Copy of letter No. 1058, dated the 26th March 1908 from the Offg. Surveyor General of India to the Superintendent, Map Publication.

I have the honour to request that the scheme for the re-organisation of the Photo-Litho. Offices, Calcutta and Dehra Dún approved by the Government of India in their letter from the Department of Revenue and Agriculture No. 355-53-2, dated the 19th March 1908, a copy of which was sent to you under this office endorsement No. 967 Confidential of 20th March 1608, may now be made public.

2. In doing so however there are one or two points which need to be made clear.

(*a*) Although the new first division consists of fixed posts with fixed increments, it must be clearly understood that these increments will not be given annually as a matter of course. It is entirely within the discretion of the Surveyor General to withhold an increment at any time, and the very large increases now sanctioned will only be given to those men who are fully qualified for them. The test of their qualifications is the efficiency of the departments under their charge.

(*b*) It is not proposed to reduce any man's pay under the new rules, except for inefficiency or misconduct, but promotion in future will depend on the work done by each man, and will not be given automatically for length of service only, as has so often happened in the past. It is my hope that the prospects of promotion which are now held out will increase the men's interect in their work, and will be an incentive to them to do their best.

(*c*) Officiating promotions which are in effect on 1st April 1908, will be allowed to continue until the lapse, but in future no officiating promotions will be made except in special cases, when the absence of one man throws extra work or responsibility on another, in which case acting allowances may be granted by the Surveyor General.

(*d*) All recommendations for increases or decreases of pay will be made by the Assistant Surveyor General in charge Photo.-Litho. Office, and tbe Officer in charge Computing Office, Dehra Dún, to the Superintendent, Map Publication, who will forward them to the Surveyor General for approval. Special recommendations of individuals should not as a rule be forwarded, but recommendations for deserving men will be forwarded twice a year, on May 1st and November 1st. No man should be recommended for an increase until at least one year has elapsed from the date of his last increase. The average interval will be considerably more.

3. In conclusion I should like to impress on all officers and superintendents the great responsibility thrown upon them by the new system. It will now rest entirely with them to push on the men and keep back those who are inefficient or idle. If this work of selection is properly and conscientiously done it is certain that a highly efficient staff will be the result.

Appendix VII.

POST-WAR REORGANISATION OF THE TECHNICAL
ESTABLISHMENT OF THE PHOTO.-LITHO. OFFICE.

First Division.

Government of India, R. & A. Dept. letter No. 809-64-6 dated 25-6-21.

The Government of India sanctioned a time-scale in suppersession of the scale originally sanctioned for this division as given in appendix VI.

The revised time-scale is as under:—

2 Managers	...	Rs. 700—25—1,000.
* 4 Assistant Managers	...	„ 350—30—650.

Second Division.

Government of India, R. & A. Dept. No. 661-64-2 dated 13-7-20.

The revised scale of pay for the Second Division is as under:—

1 Post	...	@ Rs. 450.
1 Post	...	„ „ 400.
†15 Posts	...	„ „ 130—10—350.

with an efficiency bar at Rs. 250.

Third Division.

Circular Order No. 397 (Adm.) dated 30-11-21.

1. The 3rd Division of the Photo.-Litho. Office, Calcutta, and Photo.-Zinco. Office, Dehra Dun (in which is included the Printing Section) consists of 100 permanent posts of which the maximum pay is Rs. 125. No fixed proportion of these posts is allotted to any particular office. The number of temporary posts is not fixed and is subject only to Budget provision; the maximum pay is also Rs. 125.

2. No officer can be appointed to a vacancy in the permanent establishment until he has completed a total of at least 10 years temporary service, excluding service under training, in the 3rd Division or Inferior Establishments of these offices or unless, having completed 10 years' temporary service in the Inferior Establishment, he has been appointed to a permanent post in that Establishment. He should, however, produce a medical certificate of fitness on completion of 5 years' temporary service and will not then be called upon to submit a further certificate on appointment to a permanent post. Appointments to the permanent establishment will be made by the Surveyor General.

---

* One of these posts is at present (1924) held by Dehra Dun.

† Three of these posts are at present (1924) held by Dehra Dun.

3. Appointments to the temporary establishment will be made as follows:—

(i) *Direct appointments of men without special qualifications.* Such men will be paid from Rs. 15 to 25 according to qualifications and will be shown as under training Service while under training will not count for leave or pension and will continue until the man is sufficiently trained to be placed in one of the five classes (*vide* para. 4). The normal maximum period of training will be one year.

(ii) *Direct appointments of men with special qualifications.* Such men will not be considered as under training and will be placed at once in one of the five classes. They may be paid at any rate that the Surveyor General may fix.

(iii) *Promotions from the inferior temporary establishments.* Such men will be placed at once in one of the five classes. Appointments under (*ii*) and (*iii*) will be made by the Surveyor General Appointments under (*i*) will be made by the Director.

4. The 3rd Division of these offices is divided into 5 classes as under:—

Class 1 on Rs. $36—\dfrac{8}{2}—125$ per mensem.

,, 2 ,, ,, $32—\dfrac{6}{2}—100$,, ,,

,, 3 ,, ,, $28—\dfrac{4}{2}— 80$,, ,,

,, 4 ,, ,, $25—\dfrac{3}{2}— 60$,, ,,

,, 5 ,, ,, $15—\dfrac{2}{2}— 45$,, ,,

The rates of increment are maxima and will only be given for continuous good work of a high order; they may be reduced to any extent or withheld.

On classification an officer will normally be given the minimum rate of his class or his previous pay whichever is greater. His first increment will be given on the 1st April following the completion of 2 years' classified service and may be proportionately increased to allow for the period in excess of 2 years. All other normal increments will date from 1st April. Normal increments for officers on the temporary establishment will be sanctioned by the Director a copy of such sanction being sent to the Surveyor

General for information. Normal increments for officers on the permanent establishment and all special increments will be sanctioned by the Surveyor General. All classifications will be sanctioned by the Surveyor General.

5. Directors will submit their recommendations for increments to the Surveyor General's Office by 1st January of each year. These recommendations will be accompanied by copies of sanction to increments of men on the temporary establishment.

6. Directors have the power to dismiss, discharge, reduce and accept resignation of all officers on the temporary establishment. Casses of dismissal or discharge of such officers with over 5 years' service should however first be referred to the Surveyor General.

7. Continuous service on the temporary establishment (excluding service under training) if followed by permanent service will count for pension.

INFERIOR ESTABLISHMENT.

Memo.
No. 1228,
dated
24-2-21
from O. C.,
S. G. O. and
M. P. O.
Order
No. 1512,
dated
8-6-22.

The Surveyor General has sanctioned the following scale of pay for the Inferior Establishment (excluding office servants) of the Photo.-Litho. Office and the Photo.-Zinco. Office.

$$\text{Rs. } 14 - \frac{Nil}{2} \text{ to } 1\tfrac{1}{2} - \text{Rs. } 30$$

with efficiency bar at Rs. 25.

2. Subject to his approval, a promising apprentice who, after a year's service, turns out a good pressman may, however be granted a promotion to Rs. 15.

Appendix VIII.

ORDERS RELATING TO THE GENERAL WORKING
OF THE PHOTO.-LITHO. OFFICE.

Main Office.

1. The main office is under the direct supervision of the O. C., P. L. O., and consists of the Head Clerk, 1 Establishment Clerk, 1 Bill Clerk, 1 Cashier, 1 accounts Clerk, 1 Despatcher, 1 Typist, 1 Map Clerk, and 1 General Assistant.

2. The Head Clerk exercises general control over the clerks and 15 menials, *viz.*, 1 Jemadar, 1 Naib Jemadar, 1 Durwan, 1 Bank Peon, 1 Farash, 4 Peons, 1 Duftry, 4 Sweepers and 1 Mali.

3. The office receives, deals with and disposes of the following, in communication with the technical sections, but through the O. C., P. L. O.

    (*a*) Correspondence, letters, files and orders (including Correspondence. Register Slips) regarding reproduction of maps, &c., and maintains records of these methodically.

    (*b*) Accounts, prepares salary bills, overtime bills, contingent bills, &c., and disburses the amounts.

    (*c*) Periodical returns and accounts.

    (*d*) Establishment cases, *e.g.* appointments leave, Accounts. promotion, pension, &c.

Office Routine.

II.—Circulation of Maps and Files between Offices.

    (*a*) *Ordinary files unaccompanied by original drawings*:—Ordinary files, unaccompanied by original drawings, when passed between offices, must be received by the office for which they are destined up to 3-30 P.M. (on Saturday 1-30 P.M.).

    (*b*) *Urgent files unaccompanied by original drawings*:—Urgent files that are not confidential and are unaccompanied by original drawings must be received up to 4 P.M. (on Saturdays 2 P.M.).

    (*c*) *Originals, confidential files and files that contain cheques and money orders*:—Original drawings and their accompanying files, confidential files and files that contain cheques or money orders will not be taken over by any office after 3-30 P.M. (on Saturdays 1-30 P.M.) except under special arrangements.

(*d*) *Printed copies sent from the Photo.-Litho. Office to the Map Record and Issue Office*:—In the case of originals sent to the Map Record and Issue Office to be stored, the latest hour for receipt in the Map Record and Issue Office is 3 P.M. (1 P.M. on Saturdays).

Copies sent from the Photo.-Litho. Office to the Map Record and Issue Office for stock or despatch will be received up to 3-30 P.M. (1-50 P.M. on Saturdays) but unless special arrangements are made they cannot be despatched the same day by the Map Record and Issue Office unless they are received before noon. In urgent cases the Photo.-Litho. Office should warn the Map Record and Issue Office to make special arrangements.

(*e*) *Cases for despatch not to be allowed to accumulate*:— Files and maps should be passed on to other offices for which they are destined as soon as they are ready for despatch throughout the day and should not be allowed to accumulate until late in the day.

Files and maps that are not ready until it is too late to despatch them should be passed on at 10 A.M. next morning and dealt with immediately.

III.—Periodical Returns.

The following is a Statement of Returns, due to the Director, Map Publication :—

STATEMENT OF PHOTO.-LITHO. OFFICE RETURNS DUE TO MAP PUBLICATION OFFICE.

	Nature of Statement.	Date on which Return must reach M. P. O.	Remarks.
	Monthly.		
1.	Progress Report of P. L. O. ...	1st week of the following month.	
2.	Statement of charges incurred in overtime.	Ditto.	
3.	Abstract Statement of Expenditure (O. 50.)	1st week of the second following month.	Not to be submitted for the months of July, Septr. & Dec.
4.	Profit & Loss Statement ...	Early in the following month.	

STATEMENT OF PHOTO.-LITHO. OFFICE RETURNS DUE TO MAP PUBLICATION OFFICE.—(Contd.).

	Nature of Statement.	Date on which Return must reach M. P. O.	Remarks.
	Half Yearly.		
1.	Return of Estimated & actual Expenditure (O. 49.)	Last week of Jany. & August.	
2.	List of officers corrected to 1st January & 1st July.	1st June. 1st December.	
	Annual.		
1.	List of men prescribed & debarred from further employment in the Survey of India.	1st January ...	Return if necessary.
2.	Annual Indent for Stationery (Form I.)	Ditto.	In duplicate.
3.	Promotion Rolls.	Ditto.	In duplicate.
4.	Annual list of official Publication (other than confidential.)	Ditto.	
4a.	List of Jurors ...	15th January.	
5.	List of Ministerial officers, Part I, corrected to 1st April.	1st February.	
6.	Form G. (a) for Electrical Works (b) for Building Works.	15th February.	
6a.	History of services of officers corrected to 1st July.	1st May.	
7.	Statement of Actual Sale of maps.	15th May.	
8.	Return of Instruments, Books, Office furniture &c. (O. 66.)	1st June ...	To show additions & alterations to previous year's return.
8a.	Questions to be discussed at the Survey Conference.	June.	

STATEMENT OF PHOTO.-LITHO. OFFICE RETURNS DUE TO MAP PUBLICATION OFFICE.

	Nature of Statement.	Date on which Return must reach M. P. O.	Remarks.
9.	Return of Expenditure of European Stores purchased in India.	15th July.	
10.	Forecast Estimates of Expenditure on stores required from England.	1st August.	
10a.	Statement of Ministerial officers who will complete 55 years.	1st August.	
11.	Annual Indent for European Stores (O. 58.)	15th August ...	10 copies Date may be altered *vide* M. P. O. No. 3058 dated 7-8-23.
12.	Budget Estimate (O. 43) ...	1st September ...	In duplicate.
13.	List of memorials addressed to the S. G., withheld.	15th September	Return if necessary.
14.	Annual Report on the operations of Survey of India.	1st October ...	In duplicate.
15.	Revised Estimate (1. 44.) ...	15th October ...	Ditto.
16.	Annual Certificate of Possession of secret documents.	1st November.	
17.	List of officers corrected to 1st Jany.	5th November.	

STATEMENT OF PHOTO.-LITHO. OFFICE RETURNS SENT OUT DIRECT.

	Nature of Statement.	Due Date.	To whom.
	Monthly.		
1.	Map Sale Account ...	Early in the following month	A. G. C. R.
2.	Return of Holidays ...	Ditto	Chief Inspector of Factories.

STATEMENT OF PHOTO.-LITHO. OFFICE RETURNS SENT
OUT DIRECT.—*contd.*

	Nature of Statement.	Due Date.	To whom.
	Annual.		
1.	Return showing particulars of P. L. O. as a factory.	January ...	Chief Inspector of Factories.
2.	Establishment Returns ...	15th May ...	A. G. C. R.
3.	* Indents for books & periodicals.	November ...	Various firms.

IV. Leave.—All leave is governed by the Civil Service Regulations and the Fundamental Rules.

(*a*) *Casual leave.*—The Officer in charge, Photo.-Litho. Office may sanction casual leave, delegating power to Managers, Photo. and Litho., to sanction in their branches up to 7 days. Casual leave is limited to a total of 15 days in a calendar year. It is governed by the special rules laid down for the Calcutta offices of the Survey of India.

(*b*) *Substitute Leave.*—This designation has been abolished.

(*c*) *Leave on average pay, Leave on Medical Certificate, and leave without pay.*—The Officer in charge, Photo.-Litho. Office may sanction leave on average pay, leave on medical certificate and leave without pay, up to one month in each case. In the case of the Temporary Inferior Establishment he may grant leave on average pay up to 2 months. He may delegate power to Managers, Photo. and Litho. to sanction leave on medical certificate and leave without pay in their branches up to 7 days in each case. Any leave in excess of one month requires the sanction of the Director, Map Publication.

APPOINTMENT AND DISCHARGE.

The O. C., P. L. O. is authorised to appoint and discharge menials in the Temporary Inferior Establishmem for the D. M. P. The sanction of the D. M. P. is required in respect of othere stablishments except in the posts of Head Clerk, 1st and 2nd Divisions Technical, in which cases the sanction of the S. G. should be asked for through the D. M. P.

*D. M. P's sanction required before indent is prepared.

INCREMENT.

All increments to the pay of the technical 2nd division temporary 3rd division and clerical 2nd and 3rd divisions and Inferior Establishment are sanctioned by the D. M. P. and in other cases the sanction of the S. G. is required; S. G.'s sanction is required for special increments.

PENSION AND GRATUITY.

All cases of retirements are governed by the C. S. R.

APPENDIX IX.
MISCELLANEOUS ORDERS.

1. *Injuries to fair sheets.*—Any serious blemish or injury to a fair sheet should be noted, dated and initialled in blue pencil on the margin or on the back of the fair sheet by a responsible officer at the time the blemish or injury is discovered, and a report should be made immediately to the head of the office. Sheets received from another office or section of the same office should be scrutinised to see that this order has been complied with.

2. *Indents on the Mathematical Instrument Office.*—All indents on the Mathematical Instrument Office for instruments, &c., required for office use should be submitted through the Director, Map Publication for his approval and counter-signatures. The Director's signature will not be required in " repair " or " deposit " cases, which may be sent by the Officer in charge direct to the Officer in charge, Mathematical Instrument Office.

Mathematical Instruments should not be included in indents on the office of the Director of Stores, India Office, but should be obtained through the Mathematical Instrument Office.

3. *Breakages.*—Half the cost of breakages or of damage done to work due to carelessness will be recovered, in ordinary cases, from the perpetrators up to a limit of 10% of a man's pay.

The Officer in charge of the Photo.-Litho. Office may, at his discreation, reduce this proportion.

Enhancements of the proportion above $\frac{1}{2}$ and reductions below $\frac{1}{4}$ should be referred to the D. M. P. for orders.

4. *Accidents.*—It should be impressed on men employed at machines or presses that they must exercise the greatest care to avoid accidents to themselves or others.

Every accident should be reported to the D. M. P. with a statement showing how it occurred. Those who by their carelessness are the cause of injuries to others will be severely dealt with.

5. *Charges for work, &c.*—Work (other than the preparation of departmental maps) done for other departments or the general public, is charged for at office rates according to the amount of work done.

Although Photo.-Litho. stores procured on Home indents are not charged for when supplied to other offices of the Survey of India, the cost of all stores supplied to other departments will be recovered.

6. *Private work for Officers of the Survey of India.*—The Principles observed when private work is undertaken in the Photo.-Litho. Office for Officers of the Survey of India are as follows :—

> (*i*) Private work is undertaken only on the understanding that in no case will it be allowed to interfere in any way with Government work including extra-departmental work. If likely to interfere with Government work, a private job will be refused.

> (*ii*) The actual cost of the work to Government is charged ; labour is not to be included in this charge if the work is done at a slack time when the individual workman concerned requires work. No charge for supervision is made in ordinary cases.

> (*iii*) Officers may develop their own photographs themselves provided there is no loss to Government, that they do so at a time when the developing room is not in use for Government work, and that it is convenient to the Officer in charge, Photo.-Litho. Office and the Photo. Manager.

7. *Rules for Overtime work* :—

In supersession of previous orders on the subject, the principles on which overtime work should be employed in the Reproducing Offices under the Director Map Publication are recorded below. These principles should not be departed from without the special orders of the Surveyor General.

I. Overtime work should always be used sparingly, never without the Director's sanction, and only if it is essential to push through a certain item of work in the shortest possible time or to relieve a congested section of the office. In no case should the budget provision under head "overtime allowance" allotted for any office be allowed to be exceeded without the previous sanction of the Surveyor General.

II. The circumstances under which overtime may be employed are detailed below :—

   (a)   *Departmental work* :—

      (i)   When one section of the office is congested and other sections are delayed by it. This should occur very rarely as the strength of the different sections is adjusted to the normal requirements of the work.

      (ii)   When "drawing" or "survey" prints have to be supplied to Drawing offices or parties whose work is seriously delayed pending the supply.

      (iii)   When it is necessary to issue a publication by some particular date and if this cannot be done without overtime work.

   (b)   *Extra-departmental work* :—

      (i)   When a Department of the Government of India or Head Quarters Staff of the Army require work to be done very rapidly.

      (ii)   When a Government Office, Railway, Public body or private individual desire to have work which has been undertaken for them expedited and agree to pay all overtime charges in cash.

III. All overtime earnings of employees should be entered up daily in the "Overtime Book" to be maintained in each section but separate pages should be allotted for :—

   (a)   Overtime incurred on departmental (as detailed in paras. II. (a) (i) (ii) and (iii) above) or on work for a Department of the Government of India or the Head Quarters Staff of the Army (as detailed in para. II. (b) (i) above).

   (b)   Overtime incurred on work for Government offices other than those mentioned above or for Railways, Public bodies and private individuals (as detailed in para. II (b) (ii) above).

(*iv*)—All overtime charges incurred for work under para. III. (*a*) above are debitable to the heading "overtime allowance" in the budget allotment of the office and should be entered on the left-hand page of the Overtime Book, the entries for each month being on separate pages.

(*v*)—All overtime charges incurred for work under para. III. (*b*) above will be realised in cash from the party concerned and should be entered on the right-hand page of the Overtime Book, the entries for each month being on separate pages.

(*vi*)—The Overtime Book will be submitted to the Director for signature at the end of each month after the entries have been completed by the Section Officer and passed by the Officer in Charge.

(*vii*)—After the book has been signed by the Director it will be returned to the Officer who forwarded it, for preparation and submission of the necessary bills. Bills for overtime charges debitable to the budget allotment under heading "Overtime allowance" will as usual be submitted to the Accountant General, Central Revenues. Bills for overtime charges to be recovered in cash, should, when the work is completed, be submitted to the Director to arrange for the realization of the amounts from the parties concerned. When realized the amounts will be sent to the officer in whose office the overtime was incurred, for disbursement to the men who earned the overtime allowance and for their receipts to be taken on an Acquittance Roll Form. (New No. O. 4 R. and Old No. O. 20 R.) which should be filed and recorded in a file specially maintained for the purpose.

(*viii*)—The Chief Draftsman is responsible that the heading, under which the overtime charges are to be allotted, as detailed in paras. II. (*a*) and (*b*), is entered on the Register Slip issued **for a work.**

(*ix*)—Members of the Second Division are not eligible for overtime pay except in special circumstances and with the sanction of the Surveyor General. Special circumstances should be interpreted to mean that 6 complete days of overtime work has been done by a member of the 2nd Division during a calendar month. This restriction does not however apply to overtime work, the charges on account of which will be realised in cash.

(*x*)—The Officer in charge is responsible that arrangements are made for the proper supervision of men employed on overtime work and for the locking of the doors, &c., when the men leave the office.

www.ingramcontent.com/pod-product-compliance
Lightning Source LLC
Chambersburg PA
CBHW081519040426
42447CB00013B/3275